WHEN THE ROLL
IS CALLED

WHEN THE ROLL IS CALLED

Trauma and the Soul of American Evangelicalism

Marie T. Hoffman

Foreword by Lowell W. Hoffman

CASCADE *Books* · Eugene, Oregon

WHEN THE ROLL IS CALLED
Trauma and the Soul of American Evangelicalism

Fuller School of Psychology Integration Series

Cascade Books
An Imprint of Wipf and Stock Publishers
199 W. 8th Ave., Suite 3
Eugene, OR 97401

www.wipfandstock.com

PAPERBACK ISBN: 978-1-4982-8393-9
HARDCOVER ISBN: 978-1-4982-8395-3
EBOOK ISBN: 978-1-4982-8394-6

Cataloguing-in-Publication data:

Hoffman, Marie T.

Title: When the roll is called: trauma and the soul of American Evangelicalism / Marie T. Hoffman

Description: Eugene, OR: Cascade Books, 2016 | Series: Fuller School of Psychology Integration Series | Includes bibliographical references.

Identifiers: ISBN 9781498283939 (paperback) | ISBN 9781498283953 (hardcover) | ISBN 9781498283946 (ebook)

Subjects: LCSH: Evangelicalism—United States. | Evangelicalism—Psychology. | subject | subject

Classification: BX8785 H65 2016 (print) | BX8785 (ebook)

Manufactured in the U.S.A.   10/12/16

The chapters of this book, in shorter form, were previously delivered as the Fuller Integration Lectures at Fuller Seminary's Integration Symposium on February 13, 14, 2013. They were titled: *Speak to Me That I May Hear: Clinical Work with Evangelicals in Transition.*

"Alone" from *Oh Pray My Wings are Gonna Fit Me Well* by Maya Angelou, copyright © 1975 by Maya Angelou. Used by permission of Random House, an imprint and division of Penguin Random House LLC. All rights reserved.

To my courageous patients who have taught me so much.

To Olivia, Rachel, and Cathy

CONTENTS

SERIES FOREWORD

Fuller School of Psychology Integration Series

Series editor, Brad D. Strawn, PhD
Evelyn and Frank Freed Professor for
the Integration of Psychology and Theology

The school of psychology at Fuller Theological Seminary began its unique ministry of training clinical psychologists (PhD) in Pasadena, California in 1964. The uniqueness of this training was that it was conducted in a seminary where students received an education that emphasized the integration of psychological theory and science with Christian theology. In 1972 the school of psychology was the first clinical program in a seminary to be accredited by the American Psychological Association. In 1987 it expanded its training to include the Doctor of Psychology degree, PsyD, as well as the department of marriage and family.

In those early days (and in certain quarters even today) some wondered what the two disciplines of psychology and theology could say to each other. Some thought it an contamination to integrate the two conceiving psychology as a secular and anti-Christian science. But the pioneers at Fuller school of psychology disagreed. Rather than taking an adversarial approach, the faculty developed a variety of models for integrative dialogue, conducted empirical research in the psychology of religion, and reflected on working clinically with people of faith. Through it all Fuller has endeavored to bring the best of Christian theology (faith and practice) into honest conversation with the best of psychology (science and practice).

One of the hallmarks of the Fuller integration project is the annual Fuller Symposium on the Integration of Psychology and Theology, better known as the Integration Symposium. Each year a noted scholar working at the interface of psychology and religion is invited on campus to give a series of three lectures. These lectures include three respondents, one from the school of psychology, one from the school of theology, and one from the school of intercultural studies. In this way, the lectures and the dialogue that follows continues in this integrative dialogical tradition.

Included in the *Fuller School of Psychology Integration Series* are works that have emerged from these Integration Symposium Lectures, dissertation projects that have passed with distinction, and integrative projects written by scholars both within and outside the Fuller community. The series endeavors to both preserve the rich tradition of the Integration Symposium as well as create opportunities for new dialogue in the integration of psychology and theology. This volume emerges from the lectures given by invited guest Marie Hoffman in February 2013.

Editorial Board:

Laura Robinson Harbert, PhD, Assistant Professor of Psychology, Department of Clinical Psychology

Terry D. Hargrave, PhD, Professor of Marital and Family Therapy, Department of Marriage and Family Therapy

Pamela Ebstyne King, PhD, Peter L. Benson, Associate Professor of Applied Developmental Science, Department of Marriage and Family Therapy

Other volumes in the series:

FOREWORD

Spanning the twentieth century and continuing into this twenty-first century, one of several shibboleths in many evangelical communities is the devaluation of unacceptable, unwanted feeling. "Don't be led by your feelings," "right feelings follow right actions," and "you shouldn't have those feelings" are learned and repeated in many evangelical families and communities. Anger, sadness, pain, and urges of unbidden temptations are met with dismissive responses of, "set your focus on things above," and "I'll be praying for you." Lost to evangelical faith are traditions of historic Christianity that privileged feelings as the very heart of the person.

In B. B. Warfield's Christological studies entitled The Person and Work of Christ, he devotes fifty-six pages to a chapter entitled, "The Emotional Life of our Lord."[1] Warfield normalizes the entire range of human emotion created by God and experienced by Jesus. For Warfield, there are no unacceptable human emotions; there are undesirable expressions of those emotions.

In this present volume, When the Roll is Called, Marie Hoffman recovers the stories of American evangelicals who enacted a feelings-aversive paradigm change in evangelical beliefs and practices. Dr. Hoffman is well-prepared to write about evangelicals' lost feelings. She was formed in a home and faith community where she experienced the abolition of feelings first-hand. Her extensive experience and training as a psychologist and psychoanalyst

---

1. Warfield, "Emotional Life of Our Lord." 93–148.

has facilitated her recovery of her own lost feelings, and in turn prepared her to help many whose effaced feelings were unknown, even to themselves.

From a most unique and privileged vantage of being Marie Hoffman's husband, I can readily attest to the inconvenience of many feelings in marital, family, and personal relationships. However, what Marie and I have discovered in our marriage and in our lives is that the most unwanted and avoided feelings are colors on a palette that the Holy Spirit mixes to create in us a more perfect representation of God's healing and restorative love in ourselves and others.

Such discoveries for us have become an unbroken, experiential process extending into our fifth decade of marriage. Because we both were formed in families and faith communities that privileged "truth" and dismissed all too many feelings, our initial discoveries felt cataclysmic, disorienting—even annihilating. I was twenty-five before I understood and experienced in the caring community of L'Abri Fellowship in Huemoz, Switzerland that "the mark of the Christian is love."

Marie and I flourished as we detached from our early environments of "truth," which in fact were bastions of falsehood. Our recognition that Jesus' proclamation that love of God and neighbor fulfills our created purpose was liberating and life-giving. Life as a follower of Jesus finally made sense to us.

Across many years, Marie and I learned that love without truthfulness rendered love rancid. Truthfulness is "speaking the truth in love." Love in relationships and love in Christian community becomes stale and offensive when truthfulness is avoided. We have learned that the avoidance of truthfulness is the avoidance of the nurturing presence of the Holy Spirit in our lives. Frankly, I was forced to leave my church to find truthfulness, and to my utter disbelief, I found truthfulness in psychoanalysis—the "evil invention of a godless Jew." While Sigmund Freud lived the life of a professed atheist, his orthodox Jewish upbringing, with its emphasis on honesty and discerning all that is true, permeated much of his theory and method.

You will read a little about Sigmund Freud's beneficial contributions to the Christian church in this book. This sub-theme in *When the Roll is Called* is more fully developed in my wife's *Toward Mutual Recognition: Relational Psychoanalysis and the Christian Narrative*,[2] published by Routledge.

In a very real sense, *When the Roll is Called* is a sharing of some of what Marie and I have learned in our pursuit of living in love and truth. Were it not for our countless encounters of dystonic feelings in our marriage, I would remain (or not) the lackluster, half-invested, follower of Jesus of my early adulthood. The prevailing love of God and Marie have made all the difference in my life, and I hope this present book will in similar manner, disturb and renew your present life in this world.

For readers unfamiliar with psychoanalytic ideas, parts of this book will require careful reading and perhaps re-reading. I encourage all who dare to read this radical story of the genesis of modern American evangelical theology, to persevere, be angry, weep, and hope, as we all in unity pray together, "Our Father . . . Thy kingdom come on earth as it is in heaven."

Lowell W. Hoffman
Fogelsville, PA
June, 2016

---

2. Hoffman, *Toward Mutual Recognition.*

ACKNOWLEDGMENTS

No book is written in a vacuum. The forces that came to bear upon the writing of this book were myriad, but were prompted by Dr. Alvin Dueck who invited me to present the 2013 Fuller Integration Lectures. My assumption was that I would be speaking about the content of my then just recently published book, *Toward Mutual Recognition: Relational Psychoanalysis and the Christian Narrative.* When I suggested this, Dr. Dueck promptly replied, "No, I'd like you to speak about your next book." Speaking at Fuller Theological Seminary was such an honor that I looked at the gauntlet he had thrown and decided I would find my voice and my deep passion for the next book. Dr. Dueck is not only a scholar; he is a prophet. Many thanks for his belief in this project.

Dr. Alvin Dueck resigned as Chair of Integration at Fuller that year, and the baton was handed to my gifted colleague and friend, Dr. Brad Strawn. His capable handling of that conference as well as his belief in the riches that can accrue through interdisciplinary research between psychoanalysis and theology, supported me as I worked on this project.

The response that I received from Christians who read my chapters or heard my talks based on this material, warmed my heart and spurred me on to complete this book. Many said that for the first time their church experience finally made sense.

My appreciation goes to several people who worked to polish the manuscript with their literary skill, not the least being

Kristopher Spring, who had piloted me through the shoals of my first book while he was editor at Routledge. My dear and trusted office administrator, Justine Myers, typed, formatted, and patiently chiseled the manuscript to its current form. Without this efficient and responsible help, I would yet be at my word processor.

I saved my dearest acknowledgement for my husband of forty-one years, Dr. Lowell Hoffman. My colleague, soulmate, sounding board, exquisite editor, and friend, shared his idea for the title of the book and I fell in love with it. Beyond the title, the whole book is filled with his touch and supportive love. I cannot thank him enough for being in my life.

1

A THEOLOGY FORGED IN TRAUMA

It had been a lengthy train ride from my parents' mission post in Marseille, France, to Luxemburg Airport. I was seventeen, and anxious about the numerous transfers required to travel to my first year of college in South Carolina. Making matters worse was the high fever that I had developed. When the plane landed at JFK, I made my way to LaGuardia for the last flight, very ill and quite ready to arrive at school and check into the infirmary. To my dismay, my flight was cancelled; I would need to wait for a later flight.

I remember feeling such a sense of aloneness: I was sick and had little money and my only family was my parents in Marseilles. Materializing out of nowhere, a curmudgeonly old man shuffled slowly toward me, carefully lowering himself into a nearby seat. After a minute or two, hands leaning on his cane, he turned and said, "You know, God loves you." I don't recall anything else he said, certainly no Four Spiritual Laws or Romans Road. He soon stood up and left. What I do remember is that my suffering had been witnessed and words of recognition had been spoken that I could hear, that I desperately needed to hear, that morning in the fall of 1970.

Just like me on that fall morning, despondent evangelicals—lonely, suffering, and eager to hear words of comfort—wander into psychotherapists' offices, counseling centers, and rehabs, known, yet unknown, in their bustling church metroplexes. In spite of myriad church-based focus groups, Bible study groups, fellowship groups, and even retreats promising the latest practical tools to healthier living, the struggling evangelical's cry is echoed in these words by Maya Angelou:

> Lying, thinking last night
> How to find my soul a home
> Where water is not thirsty
> And bread loaf is not stone.
> I came up with one thing
> And I don't believe I'm wrong
> That nobody, but nobody
> can make it out here alone . . .
> Now if you listen closely
> I'll tell you what I know
> Storm clouds are gathering
> The wind is gonna' blow
> The race of man is suffering
> And I can hear the moan
> 'Cause nobody, but nobody
> Can make it out here alone.[1]

Surveying the landscape of American evangelical Christianity over the last century, one is hard-pressed to believe that Christians once sat at the cutting edge of charitable endeavors, intellectual rigor, and scientific progress. Surprising to many is that of the 182 colleges founded before the Civil War, Tewksbury identified 92 percent as being started by Christian denominations.[2] In 1636, the Congregational Church established Harvard. In 1701, Congregational clergy persuaded the General Court of Connecticut

1. Angelou, *Complete Collected Poems*, 74.
2. Tewksbury, *Founding of American Colleges*.

to vote an "'Act for Liberty to erect a Collegiate School' wherein youth might be instructed in the arts and sciences,"[3] thus founding Yale University. Congregationalists also established Dartmouth, Amherst, and Middlebury. College of William and Mary as well as Columbia were founded by Episcopalians, and Methodists established Northwestern University. Princeton began as a Presbyterian school, while Brown was established by Baptists. Gallaudet, a college to educate the deaf, was the vision of a Congregational clergyman. The objective of all of these schools was to prepare students "for service 'both in Church & Civil State,' [that] required a basic education for all . . . Christian nurture, classical learning, and collegiate living were to be the means of instruction—with tuitions, colony grants, advice and moral backing from the clergy . . ."[4]

The impact of Christians in early American history was not confined to education. Christians were leading the way in alleviating physical and mental suffering. Many hospitals bear names that reflect their Christian origins. Quakers erected a hospital in Philadelphia specifically aimed at providing compassionate care to the mentally ill. By the early 1800s, there were eighteen hospitals offering moral treatment for severely mentally ill residents, many of them sponsored and supported by Christian ministers and churches. Research by Alvin Schmidt has further revealed that in 1887, along with a rabbi, "a number of Christian religious leaders met in Denver, Colorado, and founded the Charity Organizations Society. This was the beginning of the United Way."[5] During this era, Christians also founded the YMCA and the YWCA.

Across two millennia, followers of Jesus have responded to the call to love and edify their neighbor and thus fulfill Jesus' prayer to the Father, "Thy kingdom come . . . on earth as it is in heaven." Out of their own suffering and the suffering of others, they have recognized opportunities for the incremental establishment of God's kingdom on earth—the progressive transformation

3. Pierson, *Yale*, 9.

4. Ibid., 13.

5. Schmidt, *How Christianity Changed the World*, 138.

of innumerable shards of human brokenness into God's mosaic of redemption.

In contrast, many evangelical Christians have, particularly over the past century, conceived of God's kingdom as a future, hoped for spiritual escape, separated from the evils of this corrupted material world. They have been taught that suffering in an evil world is to be tolerated and endured here until final escape through death or rapture to their eternal reward. These two eschatological visions—one optimistic and viewing the kingdom of God as beginning in this life and consummating in the world to come, the other apocalyptic and awaiting God's deliverance from this life—offer quite disparate theologies of earthly suffering.

Tragically, twentieth-century evangelicalism was significantly shaped by a nineteenth-century apocalyptic theology. Massive personal and societal traumas in nineteenth- and early twentieth-century America engendered widespread dismissal of human suffering within most fundamentalist/evangelical Christian communities. My heart and purpose in writing this book is to attend to the muffled cries of despondent evangelicals who languish in the aftermath of personal and cultural traumas that indelibly shaped American evangelicalism's practical theology of suffering. In what follows, I will propose a return to a gospel that embraces suffering through a revival of Christ's loving, relational model of incarnation, crucifixion, and resurrection. Through identification with Jesus' relational model, I will also provide renewed perspectives on the experience of suffering as I deconstruct and transform the evangelical stalwarts of "witnessing," "salvation," and "conversion." I will explore these core Christian constructs as they are articulated in evangelical Christianity through the lens of psychological understandings of trauma and the sequel of trauma—dissociation. The lost narrative of unacknowledged suffering and trauma in the life of John Nelson Darby will be recounted. His dominant impact in the development of dispensational theology gave rise to a pessimistic eschatology that eschewed care for human suffering. Darby initiated a sea-change in American Christianity, which was then popularized by C. I. Scofield, a trauma survivor as well who widely dispersed his pessimistic theology in a United States reeling from the traumas of the Civil War and World War I. I will demonstrate how this dispensational eschatology has been responsible for an unwitting perpetuation of human suffering by fundamentalist and evangelical Christian communities of faith. In my examination of these developments in nineteenth- and twentieth-century American historical theology, I will be answering five questions—the first two in this introduction, the final three in my chapters to follow:

1. What are the general effects of unacknowledged suffering?

2. How has unacknowledged suffering influenced contemporary, American Christian eschatology?

3. How does unacknowledged suffering reflected in historic and contemporary evangelical eschatology specifically affect our understanding of witnessing, salvation, and conversion?

4. How might we conceptualize and practice psychotherapy with disenchanted evangelicals who have been affected by pessimistic, dispensational, eschatological narratives?

5. How might the evangelical church reclaim its vision to bring God's kingdom "on earth as it is in heaven"?

Before proceeding, I wish to clarify that while many contemporary evangelical Christians do not self-identify with dispensational theology, their retention of rapture and "left behind" scenarios, with a minority of exceptions, perpetuates vestiges of an overall theology that is dualistically based: bringing Christ's kingdom to earth is often obscured in favor of a preoccupation with future redemption. This dualistic influence of dispensational theology is implicit in a faith organized around a "decision for Christ" that prioritizes future salvation to the neglect of ongoing salvation realized through a sanctifying process. The diminishing of the significance of Christ's work for our present lives is one of the most damaging and distorting aspects of dispensational theology. I believe this book is relevant for much of the evangelical church and is hopefully a modest contribution toward a paradigm change in evangelical understanding and praxis.

GENERAL EFFECTS OF UNACKNOWLEDGED SUFFERING

Suffering, Trauma, and Dissociation

Suffering is not merely a footnote in life's script; suffering is the aching space between words that presses forward, in hope, toward the climax of the story. Suffering is the ubiquitous human experience in a fractured cosmos that is yet in the grips of not yet vanquished evil and death. Fortunately, for some people, suffering is met with a recognizing gaze, a comforting word, and a loving embrace. However, when suffering is not anticipated, is overwhelming, or is unacknowledged and ignored, trauma occurs.[6] Traumatic suffering is often too painful to experience, process, or bear, and survival dictates that aspects of the trauma become dissociated.[7] While dissociation can be a normative dimension of waking mentation, traumatic dissociation is distinguished by a person's "rigid separation of parts of experience, including somatic experience, consciousness, affects, perception, identity, and memory."[8] Conscious memory of the trauma may remain, but painful affect propagated by the trauma is banished from consciousness through dissociation. Painful, dissociated affect does not evaporate, dissipate, or disappear; the affect is sealed off, and potently sustains in a suspended state outside of awareness. While not discernible consciously, the traumatic affect powerfully influences motivations, action or inaction, interpersonal relating, and perceptions of reality. Dissociated affect survives for decades and even for generations. The ongoing effects of dissociated trauma become divorced from their source and are re-experienced incessantly in everyday living, often with the devastating consequences of catastrophic repetitions of trauma across one's lifespan and tragically from one generation to the next.

6. Boulanger, *Wounded by Reality*; Stolorow, "Phenomenology of Trauma"; Stolorow, "Identity and Resurrective Ideology."

7. Howell, *Dissociative Mind*.

8. Ibid., ix.

Dissociated Suffering and the Construction of Meaning

"There are those wounds that hurt our very skin and whose sting is vivid in us, in me, but there are also those wounds we share, the collective wounds that are owed to historical, political, economic events beyond us, beyond the limits of my body," writes Mariana Ortega.[9] Personal and collective dissociated wounds have helped load gunpowder into muskets, pulled triggers on lovers turned enemies, and filled pens with ink mingled with the blood of suffering. Such was the case with Friedrich Nietzsche, who at the age of four, was deeply traumatized by his father's death. "It was a crushing loss that haunted him for the rest of his life, eventuating in his madness," remarks psychoanalyst Robert Stolorow. "As a philosopher, he metaphorically captured the impact of trauma on our experience of time in *The Gay Science*, where he introduced his famous doctrine of 'the eternal return of the same'"[10]:

> What would happen if one day or night a demon were to steal upon you in your loneliest loneliness and say to you, "You will have to live this life—as you are living it now and have lived it in the past—once again and countless times more . . . The eternal hourglass of existence turning over and over—and you with it, speck of dust!" . . . If that thought ever came to prevail in you, it would transform you, such as you are, and perhaps it would mangle you.[11]

Nietzsche's wounds penetrated and permeated his philosophy, constructing a literary edifice that codified for the world such internal devastation. Ortega reflects on the transmission of trauma through the written word. She writes,

> The question is whether words that later become theories and ways of knowing depart from or are informed by wounds—oppressions, erasures, violations, colonizations, appropriations. If our words, our theories, carry with them those wounds, and we can recognize, uncover,

9. Ortega, "Wounds of Self," 242.

10. Stolorow, "Heidegger's Nietzsche," 109.

11. Nietzsche and Kaufmann, *Gay Science*, 278.

thematize, and problematize them, might our theories not be more meaningful? And might I not be more prepared to try to see the wound in your words?[12]

Ortega's haunting phrase, "the wound in your words," describes an unseen reality of the masked and unrecognized trauma that has shaped evangelical theology. An evangelical theology born of trauma, has sadly militated against "heal[ing] the brokenhearted and bind[ing] up their wounds"[13] in wide swaths of evangelical Christianity over the past five generations.

Neurology and Dissociation

Neurological mechanisms responsible for dissociation are specific to two information-processing modes. The first is located primarily in the hippocampus, which mediates declarative memory such as your memorized phone numbers. The second, called procedural memory, is mediated primarily by the amygdala.[14] Procedural memory refers to functions such as remembering how to ride a bicycle. Traumatic experience results in a dissociation of affect stored in both information processing centers. "High levels of stimulation in the amygdala, such as from emotional experiences that are 'truly tragic and awful' interfere with hippocampal functioning."[15] Such events circumvent the meaning-making of the hippocampus and make their appearance indirectly either somatically (such as through pain, bodily sensations, or sensory flashbacks) or as affective states dissociated from cognitive understanding. Painful, dissociated affect, the source of many "thoughtless" behaviors and unexamined beliefs that are perpetually present in day-to-day lived experience, is often, unfortunately, passed on to future generations.

12. Ortega, "Wound of Self," 242.
13. Ps 47:3.
14. Bromberg, "Something Wicked."
15. Ibid., 564.

Trauma survivor Charlotte Delbo described her experience of trauma and dissociation this way:

> Life was returned to me
> And I am here in front of life
> As though facing a dress
> I cannot wear.[16]

Commenting on Delbo's depiction, Ortega observes, "One cannot wear that dress because one is no longer sure of who one is: the fragmentation, confusion, pain, and sadness transform and remake who we are; they might even destroy our sense of self."[17]

Psychologist Robert Stolorow shared his experience of trauma this way:

> When the book *Contexts of Being* (Stolorow & Atwood, 1992) was first published, an initial batch of copies was sent "hot off the press" to the . . . conference where I was a panelist. I picked up a copy and looked around excitedly for my late wife, Daphne, who would be so pleased and happy to see it. She was, of course, nowhere to be found, having died some 18 months earlier. I had awakened one morning to find her lying dead across our bed, 4 weeks after her cancer had been diagnosed . . .
>
> There was a dinner at that conference for all the panelists, many of whom were my old and good friends. . . . Yet, as I looked around the ballroom, they all seemed like strange and alien beings to me.
>
> Or more accurately, I seemed like a strange and alien being—not of this world. The others seemed so vitalized. . . . I, in contrast, felt deadened and broken. . . . They could never even begin to fathom my experience. . .[18]

---

16. Ortega, "Wounds of Self," 239.

17. Ibid.

18. Stolorow, "Phenomenology of Trauma," 464–65.

Clinical Vignettes

To more clearly illustrate the phenomenon of dissociation, I will offer two reconstructed examples that are culled from my experiences as a psychologist.

Marion

Marion, a forty-three-year-old woman, lived for years in her Upper East Side Manhattan apartment. Her employer moved his company to the downtown business district, and Marion moved to an apartment closer to her work. Upon taking residence in her new apartment, Marion became prone to panic attacks. The attacks were most pronounced as she lay in bed at night. After medical consultations ruled out a physical condition, Marion sought out a psychodynamic therapist who understood dissociation. After some exploration, Marion recalled that as a young child she had lived in a town with cobblestone streets. One night, she had heard a car passing below her window. A gun was fired, and Marion later learned that her neighbor had been killed. Marion was terrified and went to her parents to calm her, but after a day or two, they told her to put it behind her and grow up. The incident did fade away. That is, until the day when in her psychologist's office she remembered it again and began to cry. The traumatic event and affect had been dissociated. The unique sound of a car passing over lower Manhattan cobblestone streets triggered a return of the affect associated with the original event. In the safety of the psychologist's office, Marion was able to re-experience her childhood terror. Her fear was recognized by the therapist and Marion could finally experience the recognition and resolution of her split-off terrified affect.

Bill

Many times dissociation does not manifest through erratic emotional behaviors, but is felt relationally and transgenerationally.

Bill was a thirty-six-year-old welder who took over his father's business. Bill brought his ten-year-old son Brian to counseling due to his increasingly anxious behavior at school. Bill had tried everything to discipline Brian, including, to his shame, screaming at him to stop being a sissy. Upon exploration, Bill came to realize that his son reminded him of his boyhood experiences of being mocked by his father for being a "baby." Bill had never disclosed this mockery, but he had vowed to be a strong man so that he would never incur these accusations again. However, when Brian replicated similar behaviors of Bill's childhood, he took on the role of the aggressor like his father and berated Brian. His dissociated feelings of humiliation provoked by his father's mockery were enacted in a role-reversal with his son, Brian.

UNACKNOWLEDGED SUFFERING AND MODERN ESCHATOLOGY

Suffering and Resurrection Power

The promise of the kingdom of God gives hope and strength in the midst of suffering. Eschatology may be seen as more than a doctrine of last things; it is the future in the present. Jurgen Moltmann has offered an eschatology of hope:

> From first to last and not merely in the epilogue, Christianity is eschatology. . . . The eschatological is not one element of Christianity, but it is the medium of Christian faith as such, the key in which everything in it is set, the glow that suffuses everything here in the dawn of an expected new day.[19]

Hope that all things are moving toward an ultimate restoration of all that is good requires faith in a mysterious God whom humans cannot control, a restoration that validates God's very character in its outcome. As Christians, we are called to follow Jesus and become more like him as we journey toward the

19. Moltmann, *Crucified God*, 16.

consummation of all things. Paul, the apostle of Jesus, describes his own experiences of knowing Christ and urges all to know Jesus in both the power of his resurrection and in the fellowship of his sufferings.[20]

In nineteenth- and twentieth-century American evangelicalism, however, this path of discipleship, constituted by both Jesus' power and his suffering, has fallen prey to dichotomization, mostly driven by the human tendency to avoid suffering. Dietrich Bonhoeffer decried a church infatuated with power and divorced from suffering:

> We want Jesus as the visibly resurrected one, as the splendid, transfigured Jesus. We want his visible power and glory, and we no longer want to return to the cross, to believing against all appearances, to suffering in faith . . . it is good here . . . let us make dwellings . . .[21]

When human suffering is marginalized, denied, or dissociated through a preference for resurrection power, trauma in evangelical Christian families and communities becomes dissociated rather than witnessed, mourned, and integrated into life experience. Unacknowledged suffering that is subverted into dissociated trauma precipitates disillusionment and a pessimistic view of the Spirit's effectual presence in this world. Such refusal to acknowledge suffering contributed to the development of eschatologies that privilege and promote separation, escape, and triumphalism.

British Millenarianism: An Instance of Christian Triumphalism

In the British Isles, hope of ushering in God's kingdom mounted after the French Revolution in 1789. Fueled by Catholicism's decline, prophetic interest in Christ's return spurred revivals and

---

20. Phil 3:10.
21. Bonhoeffer, *Meditations on the Cross*, 4.

missionary enterprises that reached the farthest corners of the world.[22]

But as millennial fervor mounted, so did denial of massive societal suffering. This denial of trauma was particularly acute in the face of Ireland's woes and was reflected in the Irishman Thomas Moore's 1826 poem, "The Millennium":

> A Millennium at hand!—I'm delighted to hear it
> As matters, both public and Private, now go
> With multitudes round us all starving, or near it
> A good, rich Millennium will come a-propos.[23]

Concurrent with an optimistic British millenarian fervor was the emergence of dire, apocalyptic visions fueled by suffering and disillusionment. Into this era, John Nelson Darby was born to a wealthy, Protestant English family who had vast land holdings in Ireland. I will briefly evaluate his personal story with a psychoanalyst's eye and provide linkages between Darby's dismissal of his personal suffering and the development of his dispensational theology, a theology that gave rise to an American evangelical theology that dissociated suffering.

The Personal History of John Nelson Darby

Family History

In 1557, Englishman John Darby was awarded Ireland's Leap Castle as a result of his participation in Cromwell's siege. Leap was the site of bloody battles waged initially between native Irish clans, and later between Catholic Irish clans and British Protestants.[24]

The brutal O'Carroll clan, into which John Darby married, had previously occupied Leap Castle, which to this day is considered Ireland's most haunted castle. A current descendant of the Darby family, noted that the castle's dark folklore is

22. Sandeen, *Roots of Fundamentalism*; Gribben, "Antichrist in Ireland."

23. Ibid., 13.

24. Freeman-Atwood, *Leap Castle*; Weremchuk, *John Nelson Darby*.

retold whenever family gathers.[25] A dungeon was accessed by a secret trap door in the banquet hall called an *oubliette*. Unwary, despised dinner guests would be seated atop the trap door and were dropped deep into the dungeon onto daggers that impaled and immediately killed them. The more unfortunate who were not impaled, were left abandoned in the dungeon to die slowly of starvation and dehydration as they listened to the raucous feasting of diners far above. The Machiavellian treacheries of the O'Carrolls, according to some reports, were perpetuated by the Darby family. During a renovation of Leap Castle, three cartloads of human skeletons were removed from the dungeon, among them a pocket watch made in the 1840s.[26] This castle—along with the thousands of acres upon which it was situated—was inherited by John Nelson Darby's father in 1823, and the young John Darby would from time to time visit here. To this day, paranormal investigators insist that evil inhabits Leap Castle.

A present-day Darby descendant, Freeman-Attwood presents the Darby family in a favorable light. She does not address the English usurping of Irish land, nor the disparity between Darby wealth and the abject poverty of the surrounding Irish populace, many of whom died of starvation during the first Irish famine of the middle 1700s and the second in the middle 1800s.[27]

John's maternal ancestors, the Vaughns, emigrated from England to the American colonies where they lived in Philadelphia. The Vaughns socialized with Benjamin Franklin and supported the American Revolution. They were Unitarian, humanistic, and socially progressive. John's maternal grandfather, Samuel, was a wealthy merchant who owned millions of acres in Maine and Jamaica, as well as hundreds of slaves.

25. Freeman-Attwood, *Leap Castle*.

26. Vale, *Hell House*, 113.

27. Freeman-Attwood, *Leap Castle*.

Early Childhood and Schooling

John Nelson Darby was born in Westminster, England on November 18, 1800. Though he grew up in England and was geographically removed from the potent evil of Leap, he was not immune to hardship that encroached upon his childhood.

His father, John, was a wealthy merchant with a personality that was "hard as granite, deeply serious, and almost inflexible and pitiless in character."[28] Personal letters confirm his irascible, alienating personality, sending debtors to prison with little mercy.

John Nelson Darby remembered his mother, Anne, with deep fondness. He wrote:

> Her eye fixed upon me that tender love which had me for its heart's object . . . which had my confidence before I knew what confidence was—by which I learnt to love, because I felt I was loved, was the object of that love which had its joy in serving me—which I took for granted must be; for I had never known anything else at all.[29]

Darby continues elsewhere:

> I have long, I suppose, looked at the portrait of my mother, who watched over my tender years with that care which only a mother knows how to bestow. I can just form some imperfect thought of her looks, for I was early bereft of her.[30]

Young John Darby erroneously believed that his mother Anne died when he was five or six years old. However, extant records suggest that Anne was banished by her husband at John's tender age, and John would never see her again.

At the age of eleven, John left home and was enrolled in a boarding school not far from his father's residence. Discipline was severe there, in keeping with the times. Upon graduation at the age of fourteen, John traveled alone to Dublin, where he attended

28. Weremchuk, *John Nelson Darby*, 25.

29. Ibid., 26.

30. Ibid., 26.

Trinity College. Leaving home was difficult for John, in spite of the reality of no connection to his mother and little to none with his father. He recollects his pain in a letter written at age sixty-nine: "I remember yet my desolation once on leaving home."[31] John graduated from Trinity College and returned to England only briefly to enroll in the study of law. Returning to Ireland, he was appointed to the Irish bar.

Young Adulthood

John Darby's course of life changed at the age of twenty-one, which he understood as the point of his conversion. He left law, entered Anglican ministry, and was ordained to holy orders in 1824. This change of career enraged John's father, who promptly disinherited him. Darby devoted himself to minister to the poor Catholic populace of Calary, Ireland. Living psychologically in two worlds—one of Catholic Ireland and the other of Protestant Great Britain—Darby sympathized with the poor Irish Catholics and evangelized them with passion. Clergy were at this time seeing 600 to 800 Irish Catholic conversions to the Anglican Church each week, prompted in part by attempts of Irish Catholics to escape discrimination and be granted civil rights. In response to these pragmatic conversions, Archbishop Magee directed as a precondition for acceptance into the Anglican Communion that conversions must be accompanied by oaths of allegiance to the British Crown. This directive was particularly noxious to Darby, who responded by promptly abandoning his orders in the Anglican Church while continuing his ministry among the people of Calary whom he loved.[32]

For the seven years that followed his conversion, John had no peace about his spiritual state and suffered a spiritual depression during which he read Psalm 88 continuously:

31. Ibid., 30.
32. Ibid; Turner, *Unknown and Well Known*.

1 O lord God of my salvation, I have cried day and night before thee:

2 Let my prayer come before thee: incline thine ear unto my cry;

3 For my soul is full of troubles: and my life draweth nigh unto the grave.

4 I am counted with them that go down into the pit: I am as a man that hath no strength:

5 Free among the dead, like the slain that lie in the grave, whom thou rememberest no more: and they are cut off from thy hand. [Keep in mind Leap Castle's dungeon]

6 Thou hast laid me in the lowest pit, in darkness, in the deeps.

7 Thy wrath lieth hard upon me, and thou hast afflicted me with all thy waves. Selah.

8 Thou hast put away mine acquaintance far from me; thou hast made me an abomination unto them: I am shut up, and I cannot come forth.

9 Mine eye mourneth by reason of affliction: Lord, I have called daily upon thee, I have stretched out my hands unto thee.

10 Wilt thou shew wonders to the dead? shall the dead arise and praise thee? Selah.

11 Shall thy lovingkindness be declared in the grave? or thy faithfulness in destruction?

12 Shall thy wonders be known in the dark? and thy righteousness in the land of forgetfulness?

13 But unto thee have I cried, O Lord; and in the morning shall my prayer prevent thee.

14 Lord, why castest thou off my soul? why hidest thou thy face from me?

15 I am afflicted and ready to die from my youth up: while I suffer thy terrors I am distracted.

16 Thy fierce wrath goeth over me; thy terrors have cut me off.

17 They came round about me daily like water; they compassed me about together.

18 Lover and friend hast thou put far from me, and mine acquaintance into darkness.[33]

33. Ps. 88.

This psalm provided words to describe John Darby's agonizing depression, and the first verse became his only ray of hope, "Oh Lord God of my salvation, I have cried day and night before thee: let my prayer come before thee: Incline thine ear unto my cry."

In 1827, during a three-month convalescence for a leg injury, Darby pondered his faith and theology, reflecting on his feelings of bondage and suffering that were unremitting, even after his experience of conversion that he questioned. Darby re-evaluated his beliefs concerning the church and its role in the world and found in his reformulations a feeling of freedom that he had never before felt. He emerged from his convalescence with radical theological formulations that within a decade became widely known as "dispensationalism." He would help found the Plymouth Brethren and, with ardent disciples, would promote and popularize radical changes in Christian praxis. Freed from his many years of anguish, Darby penned "The Call." Two stanzas distill the theological formulations that offered him relief:

> What powerful, mighty Voice, so near
> Calls me from earth apart
> Reaches, with tones so still, so clear
> From th'unseen world, my heart?
> Yes, then 'twas faith—Thy word; but now
> Thyself my soul draw'st nigh,
> My soul with nearer thoughts to bow
> Of brighter worlds on high.[34]

Darby's Theology: Synopsis

I will cull from Darby's voluminous writings a list of salient propositions that framed the evolution of dispensationalism. They are:

1. Literal hermeneutic of Scripture;

2. Divine dispensations and administrations;

---

34. Weremchuk, *John Nelson Darby*, 57.

3. Separate redemptive trajectories for Israel and the church, and a future for national Israel;

4. A spiritual, universal church;

5. Premillenialism and the imminent return of Christ. [35]

Darby's Theology: Evidences of Dissociated Suffering

While psychological analyses of historic personalities must be done with humility and tentativeness, such assessments are essential, particularly when the impact of a person has far-reaching consequences. In her analysis of the tragic lives and artistic works of Poe, Wharton, Magritte, Hitchcock, and Bergman, Lenore Terr contends that an artistic product (painting, music, writing, etc.) "will reflect the trauma in two ways: in the literal re-creation of the artist's experience, and in the establishment of a tone of trauma . . ."[36] A work of art is created by the traumatized artist to master the pain of the trauma, to render it tolerable even if denied or projected. I will examine specific evidences of the dissociated pain of John Darby's traumas that attracted him to the ideas that he systematized or created and that became the foundation of his theological writings.

Darby's personal experiences and inherited transgenerational traumas collectively indicate the probability of the young and utterly defenseless John Darby's development of dissociation. Abandonment by mother, rejection by father, lack of nurture and parental guidance, and repeated disillusionments with church and country are all superimposed on a family history of unspeakable evil and were undoubtedly congealed into "private dramas of great significance and pain."[37] Charles Strozier, psychoanalyst and researcher, finds such suffering to be fertile ground for apocalyptic thinking. Diane Perlman, in her studies on terrorism, affirms as

35. Sawyer, *Dispensationalism*, 1–29.

36. Terr, "Childhood Trauma," 1.

37. Strozier, *Apocalypse*, 3.

well that suffering may begin an apocalyptic cycle: "Suffering; desire for compassion; reaching for help; help fails; dejection, despair and rage; transformation from victim to master of fate . . ."[38]

John Darby's painful story chronicles massive empathic failures encapsulated in his testimony of transformation: "I have always been alone, but I bless God for it."[39] Profound suffering is also detectable in Darby's seven-year preoccupation with Psalm 88 in which melancholia and thoughts of death dominated. It is noteworthy that Psalm 88 depicts being in a pit of death: "Thou hast laid me in the lowest pit, in darkness, in the deeps." Darby's familial relationship to the history of Leap Castle likely contributed to anguish over his family's blood-guiltiness.

Mortimer Ostow's research on anti-Semitic violence suggested that suicidal feelings may be linked with apocalyptic thinking as a means of "displacing the violence outward."[40] Darby's youthful formation may also have given rise to a manic defense, where feverish productivity to find control defends against pain. To compensate for feelings of devastating loss and powerlessness, Darby may have experienced delusional grandeur because of God's special revelation (of dispensational theology) to him: "what God has with infinite graciousness revealed to me."[41]

Darby's personal experience of intimacy with Christ stands in abject contrast to his childhood isolation, except for the foreshortened intimacy with his mother up to age five when she was taken from him, never to be seen again. Darby never married nor had children. He writes, "I have long, I suppose, looked at the portrait of my mother. . . . Is Christ's picture in the Word less precious to me? He [too] was taken early from man's sight."[42] He laments his ingratitude for his mother's love "which I took for granted"[43] and

38. Perlman, "Intersubjective Dimensions," 17–18.

39. Darby, *Letters of J. N. D., vol. III*, 208.

40. Ostow, "Myth and Madness," 27.

41. Darby, "Reflections upon the Prophetic Inquiry."

42. Darby, "Irrationalism of Infidelity."

43. Ibid.

associates this sorrow to his "ingratitude toward Christ."[44] John's lament for his ingratitude as a five-year-old may be understood as a "moral defense" in which the child sees itself as bad, and mother is viewed with perfection to defend against certain anger in reaction to mother's absence. Spurred by primary caretaker unavailability and John's incapacity to process distressing emotion at age five, he could not have prepared for, mourned, and found comfort for his mother's disappearance. Such tragic circumstances usually result in a person's developmental arrest that prevents the person from achieving adult capacities to experience "mixed feelings." Young Darby would not have been able over time to develop more mature ambivalent feelings of both fondness for his mother and the sense of betrayal at her loss. His later adult life reflects a pervasive pattern of splitting into "all good" and "all bad," as exemplified both in his theology and in his tempestuous relationships with fellow believers. Darby's splitting into good and bad is evident in a letter that bespeaks his adaptation to trauma:

> I had the kindest letter from Mr. _____, but . . . he has not long ago lost his wife . . . and that though bowing to the Lord he was dreadfully overwhelmed by it. We are in a world of sorrow, dear _____, . . . Only yesterday again I received an account of another tie broken, and one, a daughter, left alone desolate; but all this is good for us, it makes us feel our rest is not here, and young as you are you can learn this. Your very leaving home has begun the tale for you; it did once for me. I remember yet my desolation once on leaving it. "Stranger" is a word sin has brought in. In Latin and in more learned languages it means an enemy; such is man. In heaven none can or will be a stranger there, nor any stranger to Him.[45]

In this letter, Darby's theological distinction between a bad earth and a good heaven is clearly discernible.

Darby had no relationship with his father, and was disinherited by him. His attempt to visit his father in 1831 procured his

---

44. Weremchuk, *John Nelson Darby*, 36.

45. Darby, *Letters of J. N. D.*, vol. II, 44–45.

father's brief audience to be asked where he came from and where he was going. With this, the visit was adjourned.[46] Psychoanalyst Ruth Stein remarks that "when the son incurs his father's contempt by openly showing his . . . need to be loved by his father, all that is left for the son is to identify with the annihilating, contemptuous [father] figure."[47] God seems to have become for Darby what Stein further described as a "(1) father of mimetic entitlement who empowers his son(s) by granting them their identificatory love and idealization of him, and (2) the Father, spelled with a capital letter who demands capital punishment."[48] For Darby, God was the father who finally facilitated his earthly ambitions, but in a categorical split of good and bad, God was also the Father who sends suffering and calamity for growth and damns ungrateful souls to hell.

It is inconceivable that Darby, a child of British privilege, could live in an Ireland so plagued by poverty and famine and not experience guilt over his privilege. He was born into British aristocracy that had usurped Irish land. This aristocracy typically lived in England and received large sums of rent from tenants in Ireland. Between 1801 and 1845, 114 commissions and sixty-one committees investigated conditions in Ireland and "without exception their findings prophesied disaster; Ireland was on the verge of starvation, her population rapidly increasing, three-quarters of her laborers unemployed, housing conditions appalling and the standard of living unbelievably low."[49] Weremchuk and Field document Darby's devoted care for the Irish Catholics during his Anglican priesthood; however, upon developing his dispensational doctrines, his concern for human suffering dramatically disappeared.[50] In the years preceding the Irish famine of 1845—a famine of proportions to implicate the English with a charge of genocide—Darby traveled extensively outside of the British Isles,

46. Field, *John Nelson Darby*.

47. Stein, "Vertical Mystical Homoeros," 47.

48. Ibid., 47.

49. Woodham-Smith, *Great Hunger*, 31.

50. Weremchuk, *John Nelson Darby*; Field, *John Nelson Darby*.

spending much time in Switzerland, preparing his first series of prophetic lectures that he delivered in 1840 in Geneva.[51] Returning to London briefly in 1843, he journaled, "I felt myself a stranger and much more at home in Switzerland than here."[52] Darby returned briefly to Plymouth, England, home to his Brethren congregation, but only dutifully to address severe controversy among the Brethren. Darby's apparent personal internal splitting of good and bad were matched by bitter dissensions that culminated in a congregational split. Darby excommunicated B. W. Newton and his followers—even Georg Mueller.[53]

CONCLUSION

Darby, whose hope in parents and church alike had been dashed, came to comprehend and perceive this world as evil and set his hopes single-mindedly upon heaven and the life to come. Human suffering was for Darby a distraction in his earthly sojourn, badness not to be dwelt upon, a mere reminder to "turn one's eyes above" where all goodness dwells. Darby's dramatic and sudden marginalization of suffering after 1827 leads me to believe that his dissociated trauma was projected into his theology, where it remained ensconced in his pessimistic dispensational system of successive human failures culminating in Armageddon. Personal intrapsychic splits and related dissociations of disturbing affect in religious leaders can potentially contribute to theological dualisms and have become manifest in the history of the Christian church as controversies: Good vs. Evil; Suffering vs. Glory; Jew vs. Gentile; Male Strength vs. Female Need; Individual vs. Communal; Earthly vs. Spiritual; and Present vs. Future. In the next three chapters, I will reflect on several of these dualisms as they are manifest in Darby's theology and in the writings of those who advanced his dispensational views. In the final chapter and Epilogue, I will

51. Ibid.

52. Darby, *Letters of J. N. D., vol. II*, 63.

53. Field, *John Nelson Darby*.

distill what I believe are three overarching categories of destructive dualisms that have affected American evangelical Christianity and will then suggest measures to remediate them.

2

WITNESSING
Where It All Begins

INTRODUCTION

For most evangelical Christians today, witnessing is about offering the hope of salvation to people so that they may enjoy eternity with the Lord. Through the acceptance of the good news of God's offer to forgive sin as a result of Christ's finished work on the cross, any who believe can be saved from the suffering of eternal damnation. As a result of the influence of Darby's views that were popularized by his American disciples—C. I. Scofield, Lewis Sperry Chafer, and Dwight L. Moody[1]—witnessing among many American evangelicals is unwittingly understood through a dualism that Darby established: hope is limited to the future actions of God on behalf of those individuals who while on earth avail themselves of God's gift of salvation and await his deliverance from this present evil age.[2]

1. Marsden, *Understanding Fundamentalism*; Sandeen, *Roots of Fundamentalism*.

2. Henzel, *Darby, Dualism*.

The etymology of the noun *witness* derives from the Greek word for martyr, as in one who suffers as he/she testifies of Christ. Used commonly as a word to describe bearing testimony to an event or to someone's suffering, it remains closely identified with the social ethic of truth-telling in the service of justice. However, the noun form that linked being a witness to suffering and justice was essentially displaced and supplanted in American evangelicalism. The verb form *to witness* evolved to its current, more dominant usage, which denotes the act of proselytizing. The shift in focus moved witnessing from an interpersonal encounter related to suffering and justice to the hard-driving marketing of a future hope. Such dismissal of attention to present suffering has drawn a cautionary note from theologian Jurgen Moltmann, who writes: "Unless it apprehends the pain of the [present] negative, Christian hope cannot be realistic and liberating."[3]

DECONSTRUCTING WITNESSING

Present and Future; Material and Spiritual

Darby's traumas were myriad. Few, if any, of these traumas were witnessed and attended to by attentive caregivers, and this absence of recognition and response most surely culminated in Darby's utilization of dissociation and splitting. Robert Stolorow elaborates on the outcomes of trauma when not met with witnessing and comfort:

> If a relational home can be found in which traumatized states and anxiety can be held and eventually integrated . . . the traumatized person may actually move toward a more authentic way of existing, in which existential vulnerabilities are embraced rather than disowned. More commonly, in the absence of such a relational home, he or she may succumb to various forms of dissociative numbing. Alternatively, groups of traumatized people may attempt to restore the lost illusions shattered by

3. Moltmann, *Crucified God*, 5.

trauma through some form of what I call resurrective ideology—collective beliefs about one's being-in-the-world that seek to bring back to life the absolutisms that have been nullified.[4]

Darby's theology fits like an overlay to Stolorow's description. Unlike the Wesleyans who saw evil in the world but believed that they could repair it,[5] Darby demanded utter separation from the present world and a singular investment in the spiritual world, even if one is in a position to offer relief for suffering. If the citizen of a town or country could cast a vote for a more just government official who promised to relieve human suffering, Darby would dissent:

> For instance: everybody says that a citizen of the country, a Christian, should be interested in the government of the country to which he belongs, and ought to vote, so as to help to put good men in power. God says differently; in many places and ways He tells me that, as His child, I am not a citizen of any country, or a member of any society; my citizenship is in heaven . . .[6]

Darby transmitted his own unwitnessed suffering onto others through minimizing and dismissing their suffering.[7] Darby's denial of the depth and agonies of present suffering is sadly evident in these words penned to a bereaved parent:

> I thank you and dear M much for having thought of sending me the account of the accident to your dear babe. It is indeed a sore trial to see one who is a part of ourselves thus taken off at one blow, and unexpectedly. Still, what a difference, to have the Lord's love to look to, and to believe one's babe—as I surely do—the object of it. It is a consolation which changes everything, because everything is changed. The knowledge of the love of God, which is come into this place of death, has brightened

4. Stolorow, "Identity and Resurrective Ideology," 207.

5. Armistead, Strawn, and Wright, *Wesleyan Theology*.

6. Darby, "What the World Is."

7. Benjamin, "Identification with the Aggressor."

with the most blessed rays all its darkness; and the darkness even only serves to shew what a comfort it is to have such a light. There is nothing in the heart but light . . . It is only in the part which has to be broken and corrected that we suffer; a touched affection, when Christ is with us in the grief, is of infinite sweetness, though the sweetness of sorrow. It is only when the will mixes itself up with the sorrow that there is any bitterness in it, or pain in which Christ is not. But then this is all useful and what we need. The Lord takes your dear babe to heaven (certainly he has no loss): what is the rest of God's dealings in it with us—with one's heart? He who has made a mother's feelings knows what they are—knows what He has wounded, and knows why—has a purpose of love in it . . . God breaks in upon us; how many things He shews—how many cords He cuts at one blow![8]

Human misery was to be minimized—swept under the rug— "just give it to Jesus and turn the page." Heaven and the glories of the risen Christ are to be the Christian's solitary focus.

Individual and Communal

Human suffering is compounded by Darby's theology, which hyperbolizes a spiritualized, personal relationship with God to the minimization of relationships with loved ones.[9] For Darby, even the well-being of family, friend, or congregation can distract the individual disciple of Christ from his or her calling: "I have not seen the Lord leave those who have given themselves up to work, trusting Him; and I have seen distress of spirit and greatly hindered usefulness in those who, through their wives or own hearts, have turned to other things to help wife or family here."[10] Darby self-discloses, "I was always a solitary soul, thinking more for, than with people; but it is good to be more alone—Most good if it be

---

8. Darby, "Afflictions Lessons."

9. Brown and Strawn, *Physical Nature of Christian Life*.

10. Darby, "Pilgrim Portions."

more alone with Christ. What a place that is!"[11] Darby generalized his own singular preoccupation with the spiritual Christ in heaven to his instruction and admonition of his followers:

> Connect your service with nothing but God, not with any particular persons. You may be comforted by fellowship, and your heart refreshed; but you must work by your own individual faith and energy, without leaning on any one whatever; for if you do, you cannot be a faithful servant. Service must ever be measured by faith, and one's own communion with God. . . . In every age the blessing has been by individual agency, and the moment it has ceased to be this it has declined into the world.[12]

Darby's dismissal of suffering in this present world, his focus on a future salvation to the exclusion of the present, and his privileging of the individual over communal experience of faith permeates hymnology and even some contemporary music of the church. Three stanzas from a century-old hymn influenced by Darby's theology commend this single-minded dismissal of present sorrow in the service of a dualistic vision of living to be a witness for things above:

> 1 I am a stranger here, within a foreign land; My home is far away, Upon a golden strand; Ambassador to be of realms beyond the sea, I'm here on business for my King.
>
> 2 This is my King's command; that all men, everywhere; Repent and turn away from sin's seductive snare; That all who will obey, with him shall reign for aye, I'm here on business for my King.
>
> 3 My home is brighter far than Sharon's rosy plain, Eternal life and joy throughout its vast domain; My sovereign bids me tell how mortals there may dwell, And that's my business for my King.[13]

This truncated view of witnessing—the King's business—as a singular calling to make disciples has visited both disillusionment

---

11. Weremchuk, *John Nelson Darby*, 155.

12. Darby, "Pilgrim Portions."

13. Cassel, "King's Business," in *50 Uncomomon Songs*.

and even despair upon contemporary followers of Christ. Many evangelicals today feel forced to deny, hide, or dissociate their suffering because it can only impede the mission of the church.[14] Their pain, their confusion, and their aloneness go un-witnessed, and they are denied present transformation of personal suffering through a genuine present experience of resurrection power. Such was the case with Olivia.

OLIVIA, PART I[15]

Olivia was a striking woman. In her sixties, she carried herself with the youthful posture of a forty-year-old. Olivia had previously been my patient for a short period fifteen years earlier, not long after her acceptance of Christ at midlife while attending a very conservative Bible church. Her primary complaint then was depression and difficulties relating to her married son. She improved and terminated, and I was mildly surprised when she wanted to resume psychotherapy. In the intervening years, I had completed psychoanalytic training, and when Olivia returned, I was able to provide a depth of psychotherapy that Olivia had not experienced with me in our previous work.

When I previously knew Olivia, I had experienced her as the most zealous witness for Christ that I had encountered in my practice. She left gospel tracts in the restrooms of my office building; in her warm, disarming manner, she had also perfected the strategy of turning every conversation to speaking of her faith. Her singular gospel message had become annoying to her extended family, and increasing numbers of her relatives steered clear of her. Olivia's husband Joe, not nearly as enthusiastic about his faith, struggled to keep up with her pace and often mocked her both in private and with friends.

Olivia's second course of psychotherapy began quite differently than the first. Gone was the zealous witness for Christ; Olivia

14. Makant, "Re-membering Redemption."

15. All patient material in this book has been disguised; non-essential details have been changed to protect the identities of the patients.

seemed thoroughly broken and was barely able to function. She repeatedly shared that she wanted to be with Christ. Her husband drove her to sessions, and she sobbed through many of them. I learned that Olivia had left the Bible church and affiliated with a larger evangelical church. She had difficulty finding friends there who applauded her vibrant faith, and she made attempts to adapt to this affluent church community that encouraged a more nuanced evangelism. During a Sunday School class, the teacher, who was studying to be a counselor, introduced an exercise for identifying unresolved feelings. Olivia was asked to role-play a child being reprimanded by a tall man who was a father figure. Upon returning home, Olivia collapsed into uncontrollable sobs, and her level of functioning steadily declined. One month later, she called me for an appointment. Over the course of many months, I became a witness to Olivia's previously undisclosed suffering, and a witness to resurrection hope.

RETRADITIONING WITNESSING

Witnessing is the heart and soul of Jesus' years on earth, for the incarnation is a story of God with us, witnessing our pain, suffering our agonies.[16] Jesus' witnessing (experiencing with us) our suffering opened a way where there previously was no way for men and women to feel and know God's compassion for all who suffer. Jesus' choice to lay down his power to become "one of us" was his acceptance of a role as witness to, and as sufferer with, our separation from God and one another. Like Jesus, our own suffering and suffering with others precedes bearing witness to hope, just as Jesus' crucifixion preceded his resurrection. Witnessing is bidirectional: while primarily being preoccupied with the suffering of the other, the resiliency of the witness also bears witness to hope and resurrection. In my clinical work informed by my Christian narrative, I unobtrusively hold together a dialectic of suffering and resurrection power. This dialectic is organized by the kingdom of

16. Hoffman, *Toward Mutual Recognition*; Kim, "Salvation and Suffering"; Terrell, "Discussion of Intentional Incarnational Integration."

God metanarrative of a redemptive *telos* and my personal experiences of the fellowship of Christ's suffering as well as the experience of his resurrection power.

My own practice of witnessing in my psychoanalytic psychology practice is perhaps best described as providing a surround of mutual recognition, and it is similar to the space of a mother's maternal preoccupation with her infant who sees itself reflected in mother's eyes.[17] Affirming, confirming, and disconfirming maternal reflections build an infant's sense of self and develop a child's narrative of personal identity. Mothers both reflect back their experiences of their child to the child and act upon these senses of their child to create and nurture understandings and meanings of expectable living for the child. Infant researcher Daniel Stern comments: "We learn we are hungry because the other feeds us at a moment when we are having a certain uncomfortable feeling, and so we then have a story that goes with that feeling: 'I am hungry.'"[18] Witnessing the other's suffering is really about their being known as well. Stern writes,

> We need to feel that we exist in the other's mind, and that our existence has a kind of continuity in that mind; and we need to feel that the other in whose mind we exist is emotionally responsive to us, that he or she cares about what we experience and how we feel about it.[19]

Trauma studies reveal that persons who suffer trauma that is witnessed are more likely to understand, feel, and develop a coherent narrative of acceptance of themselves, others, and the traumatic events.[20] Trauma studies also find less dissociation when a person's trauma is witnessed. Witnessing requires more than empathic care: Caring people often listen to a person's traumatic story, even numerous retellings of it, unaware that affect generated by the trauma is already partially or wholly dissociated and beyond

17. Hoffman, *Toward Mutual Recognition*.

18. Stern, *Daniel*, 110.

19. Ibid., 111.

20. Benjamin, "Identification with the Aggressor"; Boulanger, *Wounded by Reality*.

the reach of a caring other's empathy. John Darby and Olivia may have shared their stories with others, but their emotions, somatic memories, and unconsciously altered life narrative all remained unknown and unacknowledged to self and others.

Witnessing of suffering is necessary at both explicit and implicit levels. Witnessing of suffering at the explicit level is offered by caring persons who "as a responsive person makes recognition and affective experiencing of past traumas possible for [people] who may never have experienced the meaning and articulation of their traumatic histories."[21] Explicit-level witnessing occurs in many psychotherapies, counseling, and even support groups and personal relationships, and is marked by the empathic responsiveness and focused attunement of the caring other.

Witness of suffering at the implicit level requires an understanding of dissociation because some painful affect is not yet formulated or has already been dissociated. Grand asserts that "those human atrocities that can be neither seen nor heard in the survivor's testimony actually retain their force through narrative absence . . ."[22] This hidden suffering often can emerge in a psychotherapy relationship. Witnessing of suffering at the implicit level rarely occurs outside of psychotherapy relationships. When this hidden suffering spontaneously manifests in a professional psychotherapy relationship as a repetition of the trauma, it can be recognized and resolved, and leads to a reintegration of dissociated material. Olivia's second course of psychotherapy demonstrates this process.

OLIVIA, PART II

Olivia attended church communities that were quite influenced by theologies of victorious Christian living and provided precious little space for the acknowledgement of suffering. A "turning of one's eyes upon Jesus" would allow the trials of earth to "grow

---

21. Reis, "Performative and Enactive Features," 1361.
22. Grand, *Reproduction of Evil*, 24.

strangely dim." Evangelistic witnessing had distracted Olivia for many years from the lurking pain within her. In her present congregation, Olivia's evangelistic witness was no longer a source of affirmation, and she found herself alone with her thoughts and unacknowledged feelings. With her children grown, and her husband Joe emotionally removed, Olivia was listing toward depression. The Sunday School role-play became the catalyst for Olivia's pain to come billowing out.

As the eldest of eventually eight children, Olivia had parented each of her siblings through the hideous years of her mother's repeated psychotic breaks. One day, Olivia's mother would be a cougar ready to pounce; the next day, she would be utterly withdrawn and incoherent. Olivia often wondered what she did to provoke and instigate her mother. She was bad—her mother and father told her so. Dad was an occasional respite; at times he connected to Olivia and gave her hope. Reaching adulthood, Olivia found that her striking appearance scored points with employers and suitors. She swiftly married and divorced and eventually found love with Joe, who cared for her. Much of the second period of Olivia's therapy was specific to her relationship with Joe, who over the years had become increasingly withdrawn, and who now responded to her distress with dismissive platitudes such as "Trust God—he loves you."

I was witness to Olivia's two losses of her father, the more recent of which was his death. We learned that Olivia's inconsolable grief after the Sunday School role-play were the tears of a five-year-old girl whose father had abandoned her and her siblings to a chaotic life with a psychotic mother. This sadness had not emerged in the first therapy; my witnessing of this early annihilating loss of her father was vital to Olivia's healing.

Chronic marital discord with Joe seemed parallel to Olivia's issues with her mother, and both situations seemed unresolvable. Olivia was identified with her crazy mother and only with much effort began to realize that Joe's incapacity for intimacy was actually greater than her own. Olivia enrolled in courses, developed new friendships, and was coming to life. Abruptly, her depression returned to descend and hover over her like a thick mountain fog. No matter how I intervened or cared, Olivia's depression was unremitting. I was concerned and wondered about what I was missing or doing wrong.

What I came to recognize illustrates the implicit type of witnessing that is so essential for the healing of a person with dissociated trauma. I was excited about Olivia's growth; however, in my joy over her "resurrection," I was blind to the little five-year-old girl who was still suffering. I might even suggest that Olivia actually helped me relocate my own suffering self-states that I wanted to dismiss. After numerous appointments with Olivia, and my own self-analysis, I came to the discovery that I was experiencing what she had experienced as a child: powerlessness. This could not be known to me until I identified my own feelings. I was powerless to help Olivia, and I was concerned—even frightened—that I was doing something wrong or missing something. In what Racker named a *concordant identification*,[23] I identified with and experienced what it was like for Olivia to be the child of a severe schizophrenic mother whom she could not heal, and I was able to both witness this helplessness through experiencing it and comfort her with a depth of empathy not previously available to me. Olivia's ascent out of depression began in this appointment when together we finally understood her sorrow, which we continued to work through for many sessions.

CONCLUSION

When suffering is witnessed, the healing balm of loving relationship revives the dead and hopeless places of the human heart: The dead are raised to life in the power of Christ's resurrection. Such resurrection is possible when a professional therapeutic haven is provided where that power is mediated through love. That love unites present and future experiences, creating a seamless unity of material and spiritual worlds in the kingdom of God and

23. Racker, "Meanings and Uses."

transforming our psychotherapy offices into healing sanctuaries. In such a haven, there is hope for restoration after suffering. In the chapter to follow, a process for restoration will be considered.

3

SALVATION

From "Bye and Bye" to "Here and There"

INTRODUCTION

My father's black, leather-bound Scofield Bible dominates my childhood memories. Several years past his death at the age of ninety-nine, I now look at his duct-taped, highlighted, and bookmarked Scofield King James Version Bible, and I feel both deep appreciation for his passionate love of God and deep sadness that one person's interpretation of Scripture foreclosed upon any possibility of awe or mystery in Holy writ. For my father, God's words were definitively understood through the inspired words of C. I. Scofield.

Each morning and evening, my parents and I would have family devotions, and in deepest concern for my soul, my father would be certain to emphasize that obedience to God was demonstrated by unflinching obedience to parents, a sign that I was regenerated. The consequences of being unregenerate were unthinkable. My father regularly articulated the torments that hell would inflict upon the soul that had failed to truly come to Christ.

Lying in bed at night, I was persecuted by doubts that I had "done it right," and as a very young child, I would ask God to let lightning strike by my window to confirm to me that, in fact, I was going to heaven. After many trips down the aisle, and at least three immersions in water, I concluded that if I were still unregenerate, God wasn't the God that my father said he was, and I would just leave it there. Today, I can be amused by my memories, but I find no amusement in the torment and sometimes rejection of Christian faith of many steeped in this pessimistic theology that I have witnessed in many of my patients for nearly thirty years. My sadness is not only for my father, but also for myself and millions of others who, on a daily basis, feared whether or not their souls were secure from the wrath to come.

For generations of Christians who have languished in the dichotomization of salvation into present and future, "being saved" was the desired outcome of being witnessed to. When true apprehension of a heart in rebellion against God was accompanied by unconditional repentance over that rebellion, "acceptance" of Christ would ensure both rapture upon the imminent return of Christ and escape of hellfire, the just punishment reserved for those who reject God's gift of salvation. Although this picture of salvation has been more recently air-brushed and photo-shopped, the emphasis remains on the necessity of a decision for Christ during one's lifetime in order to assure one's eternal destiny. With unswerving certainty, this decision for salvation assures the convert of eternal, blessed habitation in the presence of Jesus who will be known face to face, and this anticipation suffuses daytime musings and even nighttime dreams. But the preoccupation with a "decision for Christ" shortchanges evangelicals, limiting their salvation experience to survival in a lower story of material suffering as they await deliverance to the upper story of spiritual glory. These hapless Christians live in ignorance of a salvation from torment that begins here and now and are deprived of an abundant life as promised by Christ and experienced through a knowledge that encompasses Christ's resurrection power and a fellowship in his sufferings.

To illustrate, I will present the story of Rachel, a patient trapped in a distorted understanding of salvation. I will also return to the work of John Darby and deconstruct his theology that propelled evangelicalism into its dualistic rendering of life on earth and life in heaven. My goal is to add complexity to and hopefully retradition the prevailing, bifurcated, dualistic understanding of "salvation." To assist me in this goal, I will resource the writings of W. R. D. Fairbairn—Christian, Scotsman, psychoanalyst, and seminarian.

RACHEL: THE PATIENT MY DOG ALMOST DESTROYED, PART I

When you receive a referral from a senior psychoanalyst in your area, you strive to do your job as well as possible—perhaps more well than usual. Such was my perfectionistic desire with Rachel, a patient suffering from Obsessive Compulsive Disorder (OCD).

Rachel was a petite, forty-two-year-old married woman, who lived a sparse and secluded life. She had been plagued with OCD symptoms most of her life, but eight years before, upon the death of her father, her symptoms tortuously increased. Once before, her symptoms had similarly increased—after the birth of her only child, Kyle.

Rachel had attempted psychotherapy two times before, with little benefit. To her credit, she located an internationally known cognitive-behavioral therapist and author, struggled through traveling to his office, and attempted to comply with his directives. She left this treatment feeling extremely discouraged. A high dosage of anti-depressants did nothing to improve her symptoms, and she became adamantly opposed to further psychopharmacological interventions. She tried therapy again with another psychologist whose treatment was more non-directive, but again she felt no improvement.

The day she first came for treatment, Rachel—gray hair pulled back into a ponytail—quietly sat in a chair furthest from my own and close to an exit, and probed my demeanor. When I asked her reason for coming, she simply replied, "OCD is what I am seeking treatment for." Rachel wore no make-up and was dressed in sneakers and a pair of jeans. What announced her difficulties was the fact that she wore her heavy winter coat through the session and left her gloves on as well. This would be the Rachel that I would see for many, many weeks.

The OCD symptoms focused primarily on rituals she would engage in to protect herself from germs. She could touch no mail, would only drive a vehicle when absolutely necessary, and had not been to church in years because of her fear of becoming contaminated and contaminating others. Any inadvertent contact with something foreign would require hours of hand washing, clothes washing, and bathing. Her hands would bleed as a result of the washing, but she could not apply lotion because she believed the bottle would be contaminated. At times, unable to be sure that her clothes were germ-free, she would throw them away. Of necessity, the walls of her house were bare and the furniture was sparse. Dust collectors would increase the presence of germs.

She would consult with her physician only in the direst of circumstances and could not visit anyone in a medical facility because that would be the most likely place to become contaminated. This proved quite problematic for her each time her mother required medical attention, which was quite often.

Her mother lived in an apartment annexed to her house and would wander into Rachel's quarters necessitating hours of laborious cleaning after mother was escorted out. Her mother was a critical and un-empathic person who cared little for Rachel's feelings, though Rachel did her best to care for her. She had to take care of her mother; it was her duty in life. No question. No dialogue. End of discussion. But she was also very angry that this was her lot. Her sister—mom's favorite—was spared any duties.

I had a very tender reaction to Rachel. She was truly a tortured person. Honest and caring, she longed to be saved from her symptoms. She had the typical magical thinking of OCD patients, which extended into her faith as well. Why had God not healed her from her OCD? With some prodding, Rachel admitted to being upset with God about this, but of course, good Christians surrender that anger to God and don't question his ways. Her conclusion was that she must be so unworthy of his care, for she had asked for years to be healed. Rachel's God-image and childhood history coalesced to afford her little hope of salvation in the here-and-now.

DECONSTRUCTING SALVATION

As a psychologist, I find childhood traumas encapsulated within John Darby's writings, and I recognize defensive mechanisms in his thinking that served to sequester his suffering and that consequently projected his disavowed internal conflicts into his theological opus. Darby's thinking was instrumental in inaugurating a major eschatological shift in Christian thought from the predominant optimistic millennial hope of redeeming life here on earth, to his apocalyptic deliverance from damnation paradigm. Darby's views marginalized the rich meaning and value of life in this world, supplanting active engagement in the present and coming kingdom of God with passive expectation of deliverance to the presence of God in the future.[1] From my psychological perspective, Darby's theological dualism of this present evil world and a good future to come was a defensive strategy constructed to minimize his daily experience of internal conflict and suffering.

Darby's writings on salvation emphasize God's judgment of sin that has been fully satisfied by Christ's death on the cross and the assurance of attaining heaven that is procured through acceptance of Christ's gift of salvation to those who believe. While the elements of Darby's salvation are consistent with Scripture, his emphasis gives me pause. Salvation from future eternal damnation for individuals who do receive God's gift is the dominant theme, an emphasis consistent with his focus on a salvation that is not relevant to earthly life. Darby writes:

> Do you think that you are going with your sins into heaven? How many sins had Eve committed when God

1. Marsden, *Understanding Fundamentalism*; Henzel, *Darby, Dualism*.

41

turned her out of Eden? One? You have committed more. Do you expect to get into heaven with your sins or without them? Are they all put away? How can you rest a moment until you know . . .

It will be a terrible thing in the day of judgment, to have had the heart closed against the voice of the Charmer. . . . It is a blessed truth, that before the day of judgment comes, the Judge has come Himself to deliver. Of course you will have to be judged then, if you do not accept the deliverance now.[2]

Darby's soteriology extols a salvation binary of earthly and spiritual, whereby the believer becomes fortified against earthly suffering and the effects of sin through a singular identification with a spiritual relationship with Christ. The result of Darby's material/spiritual split is that a simultaneous split is established between a person's essential "vertical" relationship to Christ and that person's optional, unnecessary, or even undesirable horizontal human relationships.

Perhaps realizing the human necessity of salvation having application to the present life, Darby, through even further splitting of material and spiritual, "delivers" humans from physical, relational, and emotional pain, through advocating the possibility of a form of spiritual "maturation" that ensures deliverance from earthly temptation. Darby's leap is discernible in the following lengthy sermon excerpt:

"From whence also we look for the Saviour, the Lord Jesus Christ." Now what is He called "Saviour" for here? Christians are all saved in a certain sense—we have eternal life: but in this epistle salvation is the result of redemption, not merely redemption. Practically, Israel was saved out of Egypt as soon as the Red Sea was crossed, but they had not got the place till they had got through the Jordan too. We get in the Red Sea Christ's death and resurrection. The blood upon the lintel gave them safety while God was passing through, destroying the first-born: the question between God and the people as to their sin was

2. Darby, "Christ for my Sins."

settled, still God was in the character of judge there, and He passes them by. Yet it was not deliverance. But when they come to the Red Sea He says, "Stand still, and see the salvation of God." God had now come in as a Saviour and taken them out of the place they were in, and now they are delivered. When I get to Jordan, it is yet another thing; the waters open not to bring them out, but to bring them in; not that Christ was dead and risen for them, but that they were dead and risen with Christ. So you get the Red Sea smitten, so to say, whilst in Jordan the ark stays in the water and we go through with it. The reproach of Egypt was never rolled away till they got into Canaan; and so with us: I do not get deliverance and full power in heavenly places until I see that I have died and risen with Christ; I do not get into my place until then.[3] [\EXT]

Darby further explicates this deliverance—this "higher life"—by expounding that struggle can be averted through a volitional act of "locking the door" on the suffering and evil in oneself, and a living in Christ's resurrection power. He writes:

In Colossians we read, "Ye are dead, and your life is hid with Christ in God"—therefore dead in this world. This is God's declaration of our state as Christians . . . and this is where you find real deliverance and freedom from the bondage of sin.

Suppose I have got a man in my house who is always at mischief. I cannot turn him out, but if I lock him up, he can do no harm; he is not changed, but I am free in the house. If I leave the door open, he is at mischief again: but we are to keep him locked up, this is what we are called to do—what God calls us to do. The world will not have this; it will mend and improve man, cultivate the old man, as if it could produce good fruit, because it does not see how bad it is . . . I know, not only my sins cleared away, but myself crucified with Christ, and my life hid with Him in God.

3. Darby, "Effect of Christ in Glory."

And this is available for power, if I carry it about in my heart. Supposing we honestly held ourselves dead; can Satan tempt a dead man?[4]

For Darby, a person's separation from evil both without and within was available through a second step of salvation: "deliverance." Darby's deliverance from suffering and focus on future salvation endorsed and promoted a preoccupation with one's spiritual state and isolated and marginalized consideration of any value or worth in one's embodied material life.[5]

But is such deliverance possible or even desirable? How does such a triumphalist personal orientation of being "hid with Christ in God"—of living solely in Christ's resurrection power—manifest in daily living? For many disenchanted evangelicals, the shame of never being able to achieve this illusory "deliverance" from sin and the world has led to massive denial, stereotyped or even choreographed deception of self and others, and chronic despair. Karl Planck succinctly exposes this error:

> The apostle Paul reminds his readers that Christ's resurrection, in its fullest expression, is eschatological, a word spoken in the future; when Christians claim its fullness prematurely, he argues that word becomes illusory and destructive. To approach the cross with too much faith, to stand in its shadow with certain confidence of Easter light, is finally to confront no cross at all, only the unrepentant echoes of our religious noise. Amid the creation which groans for redemption, the church must stand as if before Easter: open to its inbreaking, but unassuming of its prerogative. There, in the community of victims and witnesses, the faithful silently wait [I would say, travail] together for the Kingdom of God.[6]

---

4. Darby, "Effect of Christ Down Here."
5. Brown and Strawn, *Physical Nature*.
6. Planck, "Broken Continuities," 963.

Planck rightly depicts the present reality that followers of Jesus live in the balance of knowing something of the power of Jesus' resurrection while yet living in a fellowship of Jesus' suffering.[7]

RETRADITIONING SALVATION

Introducing W. R. D. Fairbairn

Ronald Fairbairn is critically relevant to our discussion, because he emerged from a cultural surround that had succumbed to dualistic thinking. Evangelical fervor had burgeoned in Fairbairn's Free Church of Scotland community, creating a diminished view of the human person in his/her material, relational life on earth, and "spiritualizing" lived reality. The psychoanalytic community in which Fairbairn practiced had also created a binary of spiritual and scientific. However, unlike the Platonic Christian culture in which he was raised, and the markedly secular psychoanalytic world in which Fairbairn practiced, there was no split between his faith and his vocation: His faith informed his vocation and was manifest in his desire to redeem fractured lives. The Judaic and Christian narrative descriptions of a pristine, personal beginning, a shattering decline, and the hope of redemption through healing love is the cadence that permeates Fairbairn's lifework. Fairbairn believed that a truly Christian anthropology, ecclesiology, and psychology must retain relationality as central to healthy living. For Fairbairn, relationship is what humans seek at birth, it is what we live for, and it is what Jesus' redemptive life is about. A retraditioned understanding of salvation deriving from Fairbairn's views moves away from salvation as a solely individual event with futuristic implications, to one that also has applicability in the present and in the context of human relationships and community.

7. Phil 3:10.

The Life of W. R. D. Fairbairn

Millennial narratives were in foment in Europe following the French Revolution. Darby's apocalyptic views, which fired the imagination of American Christians through the aegis of Scofield and Moody, had already captured British Christians' attention as a result of the preaching of Edward Irving.[8] Born in 1808, Irving became assistant to Thomas Chalmers, who led the 1843 Disruption in Scotland, a movement of separation from the Church of Scotland that formed the Free Church of Scotland. Though Irving's views were widely repudiated, he nonetheless inspired a millennial passion that ignited Free Church leaders such as Horatius Bonar, who attended the Powerscourt prophecy conferences with John Darby. The Free Church of Scotland propounded this evangelistic thrust, supporting campaigns by Dwight Moody in the 1880s that drew tens of thousands to meetings in Edinburgh. William Ronald Dodds Fairbairn was born into this zealous Scottish Christianity in 1889. He would become a foremost psychoanalyst and theoretician, and would invest his life in building a theory of human personality born out of the struggles of his upbringing in the Free Church of Scotland.[9] Fairbairn constructed his theory of personality from the framework of his youthful Calvinistic instruction. He integrated his Christian faith to posit a psychoanalytically informed and workable interpretation of "salvation" that begins in this present life and continues into eternity.

Fairbairn attended the United Free Church of Scotland morning and evening each Sunday with his parents, and as a young child imbibed revivalism through preachers such as Gypsy Smith and Andrew Murray. He attended Merchiston Castle Academy, founded by Charles Chalmers, brother of Thomas, the founder of the Free Church of Scotland. At Merchiston Castle Academy, Fairbairn learned that faith and science were complementary disciplines. He completed baccalaureate studies in philosophy at the

---

8. Gribben and Stunt, *Prisoners of Hope?*
9. Hoffman and Hoffman, "Religion in the Life and Work."

University of Edinburgh, and then studied theology as a seminarian for three years in preparation for Christian ministry.

In early adulthood, Fairbairn encountered a prevailing dualism in the Christian church following his participation in the momentous 1910 World Missionary Conference in Edinburgh, which was held at the Assembly Hall of the United Free Church of Scotland. Weeks later, on his twenty-first birthday, Fairbairn journaled:

> Is the religion of the average Church of today of a nature to capture and mould the full-blown life of the healthy-minded young man and woman? Or does it only provide for one type of mind? Is it only suited for half of the individual's life? True Christianity ought to satisfy every legitimate instinct and aspiration . . . [He responds to his own query] God give me strength to do my share, however little, to effect that unspeakably desirable consummation. . . . I have decided to devote my life to the cause of religion; but may it be a . . . healthy, whole-hearted, strong religion, appealing to the enthusiasm of youth, as well as to the quiescence of old age—in other words may it be a Christ-like religion.[10]

Fairbairn's lifespan devotion to Christ, even during his service in World War I in North Africa and the Middle East, matured toward a vision to impact the wider culture as a psychoanalyst. He sought out a Christian analyst—a rarity in the post-World War I British Isles—with whom to pursue his training analysis. Ernest H. Connell was a "full-blooded" Christian, according to John Sutherland.[11] As a young man, Connell apparently attended and was married in a Catholic Apostolic church in Melbourne, Australia, a Pentecostal-like church pastored by members of Edward Irving's family who continued Irving's teachings.

In 1929, Fairbairn attended the International Congress of Psychoanalysis at Oxford University; his copious notes about the Congress are preserved in his archived papers. Fairbairn carefully

10. Sutherland, *Fairbairn's Journey*, 7.

11. Ibid.

weighed his observations of psychoanalysis and submitted them to his Christian narrative as evidenced by his perception of Freud: "[I]nstead of working out his own salvation [Philippians 2:12], he is trying substitutively to save others."[12]

This Congress propelled Fairbairn to his life project of integrating what he experienced as transformational in psychoanalysis with his Christian faith. As with other Christian analysts, Fairbairn was perhaps attracted to psychoanalysis because of its underlying redemptive, Judaic narrative.[13] Fairbairn and other analysts associated with the school of British psychoanalysis known as object relations were responsible for reconfiguring the core presuppositions of psychoanalysis. Freud's original formulation of humans being motivated by primitive drive states was transformed by Fairbairn and others who understood humans as born with the desire to relate to other human beings. In object-relations language, humans are object-seeking and not driven to discharge their drive states, as Freud proposed. Simply stated, object relations psychoanalysts believe that the core human motivation is the desire to love and be loved. These psychoanalysts, informed by the Christian narrative, influenced the church as well, endeavoring to aid it in an appreciation of the complexity of the human person, particularly the centrality of affect which was lost to the ascendant emphasis on volition (i.e., "decision-making") in the church.

W. R. D. Fairbairn and Relationality

Returning psychoanalysis closer to its Judaic roots, Fairbairn envisioned the infant as born with an innate inclination toward relationship. Psychoanalyst Stephen Mitchell, acknowledging Fairbairn's decisive paradigm shift to a comprehensively relational model, stated: "Fairbairn was suggesting that object-seeking, in its most radical form, is not the vehicle for satisfaction of a specific

---

12. Birtles and Scharff, *From Instinct to Self*, 458.

13. Hoffman, *Toward Mutual Recognition*.

need, but the expression of our very nature, the form through which we become specifically human beings."[14]

Relationality in Science and Philosophy

Fairbairn's ideas have resonated in attachment research as well as in neuroscience. In a study on prenatal twin fetal activity entitled, "Wired to be Social: The Ontogeny of Human Interaction," Castiello et al. provide empirical evidence of the innate longing to relate. They write:

> [B]y the 14th week of gestation twin fetuses . . . display movements . . . specifically aimed at the co-twin, the proportion of which increases between the 14th and 18th gestational week. Kinematic analysis revealed that movement duration was longer and deceleration time was prolonged for other-directed movements compared to movements directed towards the uterine wall . . .
>
> [We conclude that] . . . other-directed actions are not only possible but predominant over self-directed actions . . . grounding for the first time . . . Martin Buber's *I/Thou* . . . on quantitative empirical results.[15]

The emphasis on relationship as the most basic human motivation became increasingly evident early in the twentieth century in the field of philosophy. An interdisciplinary group of scholars began meeting at Oxford in 1924, their express purpose being the examination of the "relationship of faith and science."[16] This group included philosophers Seth Pringle-Pattison—who was mentor to psychoanalyst Fairbairn—Martin Buber, and John Macmurray (mentor to psychoanalyst Harold Guntrip). Macmurray and Buber focused on the meaning of personhood. Costello summarizes their joint interest: "[Their] project had two dimensions to it: first, the recovery of a recognition of the fully personal from the reductionism imposed by mechanical and organic categories of thinking on

14. Mitchell, "Fairbairn's Object Seeking," 117.

15. Castiello et al., "Wired to Be Social."

16. Costello, *John Macmurray*, 137.

human persons and social institutions . . . second, to achieve a coherent and consistent articulation of the unique logic of personal
existence . . . "[17] Macmurray and Buber passionately emphasized
the necessity of understanding personhood as existing within the
matrix of relationship. Emerging from this matrix and formed by
it are human motivations leading to human actions. Macmurray
averred, "Any personal activity must have a motive, and all motives
are, in the large sense, emotional. Indeed, an attitude of mind is
simply an emotional state."[18] In this conceptualization, Macmurray
linked relational influences such as parental and cultural models
with personal behavior, offering a philosophical counterpart for
Fairbairn's psychological premises. Relevant to our discussion of
psychoanalysis and salvation, Macmurray observes:

> Religion must be concerned with the original and basic
> formal problem of human existence, and this is the re-
> lation of persons. Since religion is certainly a reflective
> activity, this must mean, if it is true, that religion has its
> ground and origin in the problematic of the relation of
> persons, and reflects that problem. In that case religion is
> about the community of persons.[19]

W. R. D. Fairbairn and Calvin

Calvinistic themes of creation, fall, and redemption emerge in
Fairbairn's conceptualizations of both the parent/infant and psy-
chotherapeutic relationships. Fairbairn's aims and process of psychoanalytic treatment likewise envision the final movement of the
cadence: the analyst's role in redemption/salvation. In what follows, I will explicate parallel conceptions of creation, fall, and redemption in Fairbairn's personality theory and Calvinist theology
in order to substantiate and demonstrate Fairbairn's contributions
to a more fully-orbed and utilizable interpretation of salvation.

17. Ibid., 14–15.
18. Macmurray, *Persons in Relation*, 31.
19. Ibid., 157.

Creation: Fairbairn

In a monumental departure from Freud's drive theory, Fairbairn postulated an infant born with the innate inclination to seek the parent not simply for survival in the Darwinian sense, but for relationship. The infant is hardwired to seek relationship, an endowment bequeathed by the parents. Fairbairn portrayed the infant's life as one of primary identification with the parent, one that is characterized by total dependence; however, he took great care to emphasize, "such total parental availability is an impossibility."[20]

Creation: Calvin

Jean Calvin's anthropology was derived from the Judaic and Christian narratives that explain how humans were created to desire relationship with their Creator. Calvin asserted: "[Every human being] is formed to be a spectator of the created world and given eyes . . . [to] be led to its author by contemplating so beautiful a representation."[21] Lane concludes, "Calvin knew that human desire [for relationship] at its best is but a mirror of God's own desire for relationship."[22]

Fall: Fairbairn

In keeping with his Calvinistic narrative, Fairbairn's inner self is structured through fragmentation. In contrast to most developmental theories that hypothesize the establishment of personality structure through growing complexity and differentiation, "Fairbairn maintained that, far from being the necessary condition for psychic growth, structural differentiation is a defensive and pathological process in human development."[23] The infant's initially intact inner self fragments, Fairbairn postulated, setting the

20. Greenberg and Mitchell, *Object Relations*, 181.

21. Lane, "Spirituality as the Performance of Desire," 1.

22. Ibid., 9.

23. Rubens, "Fairbairn's Structural Theory," 161.

stage for a personality (endopsychic) structure that is segmented and unintegrated. "For Fairbairn (1944) the establishment of the endopsychic structure, while universal and inevitable, represents a fall from grace," writes Skolnick.[24]

Fairbairn theorized that the consequence of internal fragmentation is an inner world bereft of good, internalized relationships and thus alienated from the good. Skolnick asserts, "Fairbairn's idea [was] that the internal unconscious world of objects is devoid of good objects . . . "[25] Fairbairn poignantly portrayed the infant's frustration of its "good" longings to relate by his/her acceptance of parental gestures that offer much and give little (exciting objects), or who are overtly rejecting (rejecting objects).

Humans not only become alienated from the good; they are attracted to the bad. Fairbairn described both the cause and transgenerational transmission of attachments to bad relationships in his paper, "The Repression and the Return of Bad Objects" (1943). Fairbairn formulated that one's attachment to bad relationships occurs as a result of needing to remain connected to one's internalized parents, reinterpreting the compulsion to repeat in attachment terms. This attachment to the bad aspects of internalized parental figures is a form of bondage, Fairbairn asserting "the deepest source of resistance is fear of the release of bad objects [the parents] from the unconscious"[26] because of fear of dreaded loss. Reiterating himself, Fairbairn wrote "preserving internal reality as a closed system . . . constitute[s] the most formidable resistance encountered in psycho-analytic treatment."[27] In other words, a person clings to a connection to an internalized parent with whom they identify and are loath to let go of that internal connection, thus passing the behaviors they have learned to the next generation.

The consequence of attachments to bad, internalized relationships is alienation from others. Fairbairn's theory has "for

24. Skolnick and Scharff, *Fairbairn, Then and Now*, 141.

25. Ibid., 139.

26. Fairbain, "Repression and the Return," 69.

27. Scharff and Birtles, *From Instinct to Self*, 84.

contemporary relational analysts, become the all-important interface where intrapsychic and interpersonal relations meet and together construct a world vision."[28] That world vision depicts the tragic, human condition of interior cacophonous voices of bad, internalized relationships locked into a mausoleum of internal drama. This drama becomes projected outward onto others, ultimately subverting the capability for recognition of and connection with other people for whom they really are, while simultaneously ravaging the self with "self-deprecation and self-renunciation."[29] Concluding his essay on "Schizoid Factors in the Personality," Fairbairn summarized the resultant hopeless condition of an incapacity for true connection by use of a religious metaphor: "Since the joy of loving seems hopelessly barred to him, he may as well deliver himself over to the joy of hating and obtain what satisfaction he can out of that. He thus makes a pact with the Devil and says, 'Evil be thou my good.'"[30] For Fairbairn, the endpoint of humanity's fall from grace is the devastation of relationship.

Fall: Calvin

For Calvin, a pristine human origin—marked by internal harmony, external relationship to a loving God and fellow humans, and the Edenic spectrum of nature—devolved through human agency to a fallen and fractured world. This fall was the cataclysmic event that structured a world separated from God, "the Object of our knowledge—so that love of child or nature or whatever, is replaced by absence of the sympathy or affinity that formerly aided understanding, and the loss of harmony within ourselves in the plurality of conflicting motives and emotions."[31]

28. Davies, "Repression and Dissociation," 66.

29. Grotstein, "Endopsychic Structure," 187

30. Fairbairn, "Schizoid Factors," in *Psychoanalytic Studies*, 27.

31. Shortt, "Toward a Reformed Epistemology," 7.

Calvin's Christian narrative depicts a post-fall situation in which humans are alienated from a good God. Jonathan Edwards, an American Calvinist, echoed Calvin:

> Before, his soul was under the government of that noble principle of divine love, whereby it was enlarged to the comprehension of all his fellow-creatures and their welfare . . . But so soon as he had transgressed against God, these noble principles were immediately lost, and all this excellent enlargedness of man's soul was gone.[32]

Calvin's "bondage to sin" parallels Fairbairn's "attachment to the bad" and was certainly a familiar theme in sermons of Fairbairn's youth. Across years of Sunday morning and evening church attendance with his parents, Fairbairn most certainly sang at least a hundred times a hymn composed by Horatius Bonar of the Free Church of Scotland that begins "Not what my hands have done, Can save my guilty soul" and concludes "Thy pow'r alone, O Son of God, Can this sore bondage break."[33] For Calvin, "bondage to sin" was "iniquity of the fathers [being] visited on the children to the third and fourth generation,"[34] an inescapable transgenerational transmission of the "bad."

Calvin asserted that the consequence of internalized badness is alienation from God that becomes alienation from one's neighbors. Jonathan Edwards again recapitulates Calvin:

> [Each person] shrank, as it were, into a little space, circumscribed and closely shut up within itself, to the exclusion of all things else. Sin, like some powerful astringent, contracted his soul to the very small dimensions of selfishness; and God was forsaken, and fellow-creatures forsaken, and man retired within himself, and became totally governed by narrow and selfish principles and feelings.[35]

---

32. Edwards, *Charity and Its Fruits*, 158.

33. Bonar, "Not What My Hands Have Done," in *Trinity Hymnal*, 403.

34. Exod 20:5.

35. Edwards, *Charity and Its Fruits*, 158.

Redemption: Fairbairn

Fairbairn's writing on clinical application—the redemptive process—begins with "Eden" as a metaphor for how the ego was once "pristine" and structurally whole before being fractured. Fairbairn understood "the primary aim of psychoanalytical treatment is to effect a synthesis of the personality by reducing that splitting of the ego that occurs to some degree in every individual . . . "[36] In language that mirrors Calvinist theology, Fairbairn focused on the "fracture" of the internal world, "enslavement" to bad objects, and "alienation"—the schizoid condition that underlies all psychopathology.

Fairbairn believed it was the analyst's task to find an entrée into the closed internal world of the patient and offer opportunity for a redemptive relationship with a real "other." His ultimate objective in this new and real relationship was restitution to wholeness of the split-off parts of the self attached to bad, internalized relationships. Fairbairn employed religiously relevant terms to the analyst's function, such as "messiah," "savior," "exorcist," and "evangelist." As in the Calvinist narrative, Fairbairn's vehicle for redemption is personal relationship offered by a caring "other."

In one of his clearest depictions of psychoanalytic process, Fairbairn writes:

> Thus, in a sense, psychoanalytic treatment resolves itself
> into a struggle on the part of the patient to press-gang
> his relationship with the analyst into the closed system
> of the inner world through the agency of transference,
> and a determination on the part of the analyst to effect
> a breach in this closed system and to provide conditions
> under which, in the setting of a therapeutic relationship,
> the patient may be induced to accept the open system of
> outer reality.[37]

As the patient experiences with the analyst a new, good relationship, he or she gains hope that something better is possible

36. Scharff and Birtles, *From Instinct to Self*, 83.
37. Ibid., 92.

and, in Fairbairn's words, "may be induced" to relinquish the bad internalized relationships and attach to a new, good one. Fairbairn's conceptualization of the therapeutic relationship provides multiple benefits. First, it allows dissociated patterns of attachment to bad relationships to emerge in the treatment setting; second, it facilitates joining the patient within this space where analyst and patient travail to distinguish what is the reality of the treatment situation, and what is projected from the internal world, in order to eventually mourn what will never be; and last, it creates a new relationship in which the patient may "accept the open system of outer reality."

Redemption: Calvin

Nearly a century before Fairbairn's radical theoretical contributions, the Calvinist founder of the Free Church of Scotland, Thomas Chalmers, delivered a legendary sermon entitled, "The Expulsive Power of a New Affection," presaging Fairbairn's dynamic formulations. Chalmers wrote:

> The love of the world [bad relationship] cannot be expunged by a mere demonstration of the world's [bad relationship's] worthlessness. But may it not be supplanted by the love of that which is more worthy than itself? The heart cannot be prevailed upon to part with the world [bad relationship], by a simple act of resignation. But may not the heart be prevailed upon to admit into its preference another, who shall subordinate the world [bad relationship] and bring it down from its wonted ascendancy? If the throne which is placed there must have an occupier, and the tyrant that now resides has occupied it wrongfully, he may not leave a bosom which would rather retain him than be left in desolation. . . . In a word, if the way to disengage the heart from the "love" of one great and ascendant object, is to fasten it in positive love to another, then it is not by exposing the worthlessness of the former, but by addressing to the mental eye the worth and excellence of the latter, that all old things are to be

done away and all things are to become new. . . . In fullest accordance with the mechanism of the heart, a great moral revolution may be made to take place upon it.[38]

Chalmers rendering of Calvinist Christianity asserted that attachment to a new, good relationship can persuade the frightened person to relinquish attachment to the harmful relationship. Chalmers recognized that merely exhorting a person to give up connection to a damaging relationship was futile and would result in desolation, depriving a person, in Fairbairn's terms, of the very relationship that was thought to ensure survival. If, however, the internal world of bad relationships can be breached by someone who will not inflict further damage, but who instead will offer a healing relationship, attachment to the internalized bad relationships can be surrendered (exorcised), and the previously bound person is freed to respond to a love in external reality.

W. R. D. Fairbairn and Salvation

Fairbairn's Theory

To Fairbairn, salvation from the bondage to patterns of the past was an outworking of his integration of psychoanalysis and theology. His model offers a new perspective on what Calvin called the "bondage to sin." Fairbairn's understanding of the repetition of sinful behavior does not implicate a lack of will. Instead, with his concept of attachment to damaging relationships that exist in unconscious mental processes, Fairbairn understood the compulsion to repeat sinful behavior as a derivative of the need to remain attached to internalized, damaging relationships, most often aspects of parent-child relationships. Fairbairn believed people persist in unsatisfying and distressing human relating in repetitive reenactments of their unconscious bonds to early caregivers. His understanding of the compulsion to repeat unsatisfying relational patterns in adult relationships echoes the Apostle Paul's struggle in

---

38. Chalmers, *Expulsive Power*.

Romans 7 in which the good that he wants to do, he does not do, and the evil that he does not want to do, he keeps doing.

Fairbairn conceptualized in psychoanalytic terminology the mechanism by which "the iniquity of the fathers is visited on the children."[39] The attachment to damaging relational patterns is transmitted generationally, for one persists in identifying with what is hidden to conscious awareness and then behaves toward others out of that identification. Enslavement to internalized damaging early relationships is both an individual pathology and a relational pathology.[40]

Fairbairn's personality theory can be described in theological language, and we can distill his perspectives on salvation:

1. Humans are born to relate, in the image of their Creator God.

2. Life in a fallen world invariably devolves toward psychological and relational fracture.

3. The fractured early self attaches to significant others and internalizes them, forming self and other relational models that repeat failures of early relationships across one's lifespan.

4. When operating out of these internal relational models, a person will repetitively enact relational fractures between early caregivers and oneself and nudges others to enact these complementary maladaptive roles.

5. The internal fracture and attachment to bad relationships occurs outside of one's conscious awareness, volition, and reason, and consequently wields powerful influence within the person and is often projected out on to other people.

6. These dissociated, internalized relationships and the emotions that accompany them maintain the repetitive nature of enslavement to sin and are discernible only in their effects and consequences in present-day relating.

39. Exod 20:5.

40. Hoffman, "Incarnation, Crucifixion and Resurrection"; Hoffman, *Toward Mutual Recognition*.

7. Dissociated internalized relationships and the accompanying emotions remain locked in a timeless mausoleum of unchanging sinful cycles of behavior until, as Fairbairn would say, they are exorcised.

8. The metaphorical "exorcism" of one's attachment to early damaging relationships out of dissociation and into the conscious awareness where truth, reason, and choice is possible and offers the potential for a person to be freed from bondage to sin: "The truth sets you free."

Extending Fairbairn's Theory

Human love that derives from Christ's love brings salvation from bondage to sin in the present and enables the establishment on earth of the relational kingdom of God that continues and culminates in heaven. Christ's relational kingdom of love and peace is thwarted by the intransigent nature of damaging relationships that are perpetuated from generation to generation. Internalized bad relationships that are projected onto unwitting recipients of the projections maintain a "blindness of heart" to the "other," who is not seen as truly other and made in the image of God. Saul of Tarsus's crusade against Christians provides an example of just such a blindness, which caused him to misconstrue the true personhoods of those he persecuted. The symbolic "falling of the scales" reflects a capacity to have "in-sight" concerning one's internal, unconscious attachments and true vision regarding who the other person truly is. This turning of darkness into light is aided by a call of love—like Jesus to Saul—that can open the eyes of the blind.

This more encompassing understanding of salvation seeks to bind up wounds rather than split ourselves and others into rigid categories of the good that is to be kept and the bad that is to be discarded. As one's damaging attachments to the failings of early caregivers are readmitted into consciousness and become known in the light of God's truth through the loving help of another, a person can become capable of holding the dialectic of good and bad with respect to another and can offer and receive forgiveness.

Through the loving witnessing of another human's wounds and suffering, the potential for salvation from bondage to the past and cyclical conflicts becomes more likely. The caring witnesses' loving eyes and words offer healing love and provide a new model of living that embodies the potential for the healing of nations.

RACHEL: THE PATIENT MY DOG ALMOST DESTROYED, PART II

One or two Pomeranians have been co-therapists in my office for many years. They are wonderful transitional objects and bring out playful qualities in my patients. They also offer the opportunity for me to model how I care for vulnerable creatures. Prior to the commencement of the initial appointment, I always inquire if a person is either frightened or allergic to dogs, or if they would prefer to not have the presence of a dog during their appointments. At her initial appointment, I inquired this of Rachel (my patient with severe OCD), and she remarked, "Oh no. I really don't want a dog in the office." So I sequestered Fifi, my Pomeranian, in the office manager's office prior to Rachel's appointments. Three weeks into the once-weekly appointments, Rachel handed me her credit card at the beginning of the session to photocopy. I went to the administrative office to photocopy it and returned to my office. To my horror, and unbeknownst to me, Fifi had scooted back to my office—where she felt she belonged—and proceeded to poop directly in front of Rachel's chair, something my well-trained dog had never done in the office. When I arrived back in the room, my patient's gaze was transfixed upon her foot. Not only had my dog done this contaminating offense, but my patient had stood to look in a mirror above her chair and had not seen Fifi enter. When she turned to sit down, she stepped in "it." I was aghast. My patient—referred by a leading psychoanalyst, terrified of germs and just starting therapy—was on the verge of a coronary, as was I. I quickly procured wet paper towels to wash her shoe and profusely apologized to my now traumatized patient. She was speechless. I bent down and gently cleaned everything I could from the shoe and the floor. My mind was racing. How could I utilize this moment not only to keep the therapy from terminating, but to move it forward?

I was trained in Eriksonian techniques many years before, which emphasized "utilization"—use whatever the patient brings you as part of the therapy. Rachel's magical thinking was utilizable. With a psychoanalytically unorthodox intervention, she might continue therapy. If I tapped into her penchant for magical thinking, however, I would become cast into the role of an exciting object. The other alternative was being a rejecting object as a result of this mishap. I opted to step into the role of an exciting object in the hopes that this could be worked through in months to come.

As I gained my composure and sat down, I solemnly looked at her and said, "I believe God let this happen for a reason. He wanted me to see just how agonized you really can become, just how horrible your life must be. I have hesitated to recommend that you reconsider medication, and I needed to witness your trauma to realize how profoundly you suffer."[41] She was so taken by my explanation that she agreed to a psychiatric consult, and I procured her written authorization and scheduled her psychiatric evaluation right then and there. I knew that medication was an essential adjunctive therapy for Rachel, and hoped that she would follow through with the consult. I learned at the next session that Rachel's shoes and clothing had been discarded and that many hours of decontamination had been required.

Rachel did continue with the treatment and began to form a warm and trusting bond with me. In fact, I would say that she developed an idealizing transference. I used to avoid such transferences but came to realize that for some people idealization is an absolutely necessary stage of treatment. When I suggested that we increase to two sessions a week, Rachel was grateful and kept every

41. Secular clinicians may see this occurrence as undoubtedly coincidental. Clinicians who are Christian accept the concept of Providence. Thus "magical thinking" and Divine Providence may co-exist.

session. Her symptoms were not the focus of our sessions; rather, Rachel was the focus. She has shared with me in recent times how appreciative she was for this. No one had ever asked about her childhood, her pain, her feelings of hopelessness, her isolation. She was a cipher in her family.

Rachel shared dreams in which she was alone, isolated, and invisible in a crowd. Her affective experiences of childhood were alive in her dreams. She loved her father, but when she was five years of age, he had been severely injured in a car accident. As a result of brain trauma, her father became an angry and critical person—a faint shadow of who he once was. From that point forward, her sister became mother's favorite, and Rachel found herself being nudged into the role of the odd one, the one that nobody wanted to be with. Her symptoms commenced: She lined things up, she walked around objects, she retreated into her mind in endless obsessions. She felt so defective. So bad. So unworthy. Her achievement at school deteriorated, and there was no help from her parents, only mockery.

Fortunately for Rachel, two people were good objects in her life: her paternal grandmother, who was kind-hearted and whose loss she bitterly mourned, and her husband, whom she met in elementary school and married upon graduation from high school. Apart from them, there was no warmth, no comfort, no safe place. This was her experience of her home. It was utterly unsafe.

I frequently utilize a technique to infuse fresh perspective into a closed system, into which I introduce commentary on different internal dialogues and different modes of behavior that I hear or perceive emerging from the patient. In Rachel's case, I would hear her mentally abuse herself for having failed in some way, for not being caring enough, for not trusting God enough, for not obeying God enough to get better. Then, at a different time, when we would be talking about her love for her son, her tone would soften to one of deep caring and cherishing. There would be no hint of the viciousness she would experience toward herself. At such times, I would simply comment, "Wow, what a different tone in your voice now than when you are beating up on yourself.

Can you hear that?" Often, we can find someone or something in a person's life that is related to from the more ideal object portion of the self, a part of the self that reflects the image of God and contains the nucleus for future growth. It is important for such a person to recognize what exists in them already, because they will so often say, "I don't know how to be good to myself."

As we continued to explore Rachel's history and her current life, and as the adjunctive psychopharmacology supported the therapy, Rachel began to recognize two ways in which she had come to feel so defective. First, her family had found her an apt candidate for the role of scapegoat, and she, through the moral defense that maintains the parents' goodness and accepts one's badness, had accepted that position. She was bad and they were good. She could even be their savior if she bore the sins of the family. The second way was the impact of her family's criticism upon her. After bringing to awareness how a person is hostile to self while loving to others—like Rachel with her son—it becomes possible for the person to grasp that what feels like the self is actually an other who is carried in their mind. The OCD mentation felt like Rachel, but the viciousness felt like her mother and father. Dad's tone was "You're bad"; mom's tone was, "You'll never do it right." Her facial expressions reflected the different self-states (as we now call them) that controlled her. She began to realize that this internal oppressor was not really her—it was an alien occupier, a connection to her rejecting parents. Through comparison with how she chose to relate to her son, Rachel was able to see an inconsistency with how she treated herself and began to recognize these negative states as ego-alien. The process of exorcism was beginning.

At times, I was swept into a feeling of being an exciting object for Rachel, but we both were celebrating the steps she was taking. Sometimes, I would get too pushy with her and flood her with possibilities of freedom that were beyond her capability, and she learned to tell me this. At such times, I had become the critical, rejecting object, and I apologized to Rachel. Other times, Rachel experienced difficulty with the awareness of her anger at her parents. She feared that a part of herself really was destructive. We contextualized her parents' behaviors as an aspect of their brokenness and that it was okay for Rachel to have both anger and compassion toward them. She also was able to have compassion toward herself because she so desperately wanted to be connected to the parents that inhabited her mind.

Rachel and I began to understand the meaning of the germs. Her feeling of badness was so intense and annihilating that she needed to attach it to something outside of herself—something she could potentially control. When the possibility existed of a germ getting inside her, the terror of badness returning to its original, unsymbolized location was life-threatening, and that was why she was compelled to do anything she could to avoid invasion. Equally threatening was the possibility of her badness, now symbolized by the germs, hurting or destroying anyone else.

With the advent of summer, Rachel began to experiment with removing her coat. It would be quite a bit longer till she took her gloves off. Over time, Rachel developed a capacity to utilize interpretations given in a spirit of love, and has achieved the capacity to revel in each step of freedom achieved. One day in particular stands out in her mind. I allow my mind to wander in reverie during appointments, and on this day I shared a thought with Rachel. After a particularly harsh and withering attack upon herself, my grief while watching this beautiful woman be possessed by such a virulent rejecting object prompted me to ask, "May I share with you a thought that just went through my mind?" She said, "Yes. Of course." I said, "I just had this sense that God was saying to you, 'O, my child, if you only knew how much I love you.'" In a journal entry which chronicles her experiences in our analytic relationship, Rachel writes: "The turning point, when my heart looked up to the love of my Heavenly Father, and for the first time, could fathom the existence of real healing. What is a miracle, but a work of God—some just happen slowly." Rachel could not have considered these words being uttered by Christ to her had she not first recognized the sound of her father's voice in her mind, and the contrasting tone of Christ's love in her words to her son and in my words to her. As is often the case, the entry of love into the narrative retrospectively casts resurrection light on one's historic narrative. Rachel later journaled about a caring memory of her father who taught her to ride a bicycle:

> Looking back, learning to ride a two-wheeled bike had two different feelings—freeing on the outside, but held back on the inside. On the ride out of OCD, both the inside and the outside are free. I think God made good use of that bike and that memory of my father. I'm riding the bike forty years later. My mind attaches visuals to my thoughts; it helps me to keep some order in the armory in my head. I now know that love protects me and I don't need an armory. I didn't journal these feelings because it would have become another concrete visual that would take away more breathing space. The feelings were very big. These established concretes govern my feelings and my response to things. The concrete are losing their power and credibility; the truth is exposing the fact that they are man-made and not of God.

Ridding herself of the bad was not the same as experiencing desire and goodness. The longing for deliverance began to burgeon. Rachel was able to locate a senior facility for her mother and with great difficulty moved her out. She began to ask her husband to love her not just because she had problems, but because she was bright and witty and good. She started to attend church and was exhilarated that when someone inadvertently brushed her shoulder, she was able to say to herself, "You are okay. You can enjoy this service and not get up and wash. You are safe." She was able to achieve this in part through visualizing the loving, ideal mother that she can be to her son, Kyle, and then offering this to herself. When a voice of accusation arose within her, she would picture a harsh finger pointing at the little girl, and the good mom putting her arms around the little girl and comforting her (much as I had become to her in our therapy relationship). She could then turn to the rejecting internal parent whose voice she could now identify and command its silence. Rachel was cared for—Rachel was good.

Rachel discovered desire. She realized that she desired a home of her own. The house she lived in was her parents' home, and it was filled with dark memories. But could God allow her such self-indulgence? We worked for a while on this desire, and she decided that she wanted to move to a townhome nearby to her adult son. Her son, who had completed psychoanalytic therapy with the psychoanalyst who referred Rachel to me, believed this was not a good idea. Mother had been good, but she had also felt smothering through her attempts to protect him. He did not want that kind of a relationship again. Rachel immediately regressed after her son's dissent. How could God allow her deepest desire to be refused? She lost hope. We were given an opportunity to work on Rachel's relationship with her son. Finding a life beyond being a mother to her son was difficult because Rachel had so profoundly attached to him. Could she survive if she let go of him and found a life for herself? She and her husband signed an agreement of sale to purchase another home some distance from her son, and Rachel's OCD symptoms immediately increased. She panicked that workers performing renovations would be using the bathroom and backed out of the agreement.

These were difficult months as Rachel oscillated between letting go and having the desire of her heart fulfilled. She pictured herself stepping out of an imaginary door of her fantasized home and walking into a field. With each passing week she would walk further toward a field of wildflowers. During appointments she spoke of what she was learning and reflecting upon. She began to like colors. She repaired her relationship with her son, who became distant after the townhouse incident. In time, they were able to create a new type of relationship in which they could both celebrate each others' growth.

During one appointment, Rachel exclaimed, "I was not created so fragile. Where is the frontier? I want to have the desires of my heart." I shared with her my image of her as a little girl twirling and twirling, and she replied that in fact, that very week, she had "done that."

Healing is ongoing for Rachel, and what I described are fractals of her work. She and her husband have just purchased land to build a house—her house—the way she wants it. She has even overseen the installation of their on-lot septic system! This is land Rachel found, loves, and is proud of.

Rachel was adamant that I communicate some things to you. She believes many people need what she received in her treatment. What follows is a list Rachel compiled to be shared with others.

1. Rachel is looking forward to having some messy little piles on counters and desks in her next home—just like everyone else.

2. Freedom: Rachel loves it.

3. Directive therapy focused on Rachel's symptoms, and she experienced little improvement. Rachel and I focused on Rachel, and she is becoming emotionally healthy and maturing toward her innate capacities for mature love.

4. Rachel's previous treatment through exposure, flooding, and desensitization felt just like her rejecting parents—forcing her to do what was oppressive to her. Rachel states, "Perhaps for some people it works, but it was not good for me."

Several months ago, Rachel pointed to her shins and explained that this was the height of her health when she entered this relationship with me. She gestured upward on her body and explained that she is "growing and growing and pushing the badness out." I believe that Rachel's agency has facilitated her maturation, but it is our love for each other that is "pushing the badness out." Reminiscing over Rachel's story, I suppose I have never seen salvation so beautifully portrayed—and my Pomeranian, Fifi, now passed, would heartily agree.

CONCLUSION

While Jesus was here as one of us, his scorching rebukes were reserved for those in the religious establishment whose perverse and onerous application of doctrine distracted people from love of God and neighbor.[42] The heart of God for all people has always

---

42. Matt 23:4.

been to restore us to the experiences of love he created us to enjoy with him and one another. In concert with the Father, Jesus came to us to restore us to this abundant life of loving and being loved here and now.[43] He left us here not to writhe in anguish or to ignore the suffering all around us; rather, he sent us a Comforter and Counselor who accompanies us as we continue the good work that he began: To love one another as he loved us. In the chapter that follows, the process of reconciling all things to Jesus[44] will be considered.

43. John 10:10.
44. 2 Cor 5:19.

4

CONVERSION
From What? To What?

INTRODUCTION

Life in the 1960s was a little less exciting after school hours than
it is today, especially for an only child in a fundamentalist
home. After supper and the Scofield hour followed by on-the-knees
prayer time that rotated to cover every continent of the world over
the course of a week, I would complete my homework and settle in
for some leisure. I looked forward to 8:15 p.m., for that was when
the announcer would come on Family Radio with an intro of the
night's story that ended in bold strokes of the Hammond organ
and the announcement, "Bringing life to a troubled world, this is
Unshackled." More bold organ strokes and I was glued to the dramatic portrayal of an amazing conversion that had transformed
another life through the ministry of Pacific Garden Mission. In
these narratives, marvelous conversions transformed ruined lives
ravaged by alcohol abuse and dependence.

During the summer months when school was not in session, I could listen each morning to my favorite broadcast, which

opened with, "Welcome to Psychology for Living. I'm Dr. Clyde Narramore. My wife, Ruth, is at my side, and we will be reading and discussing some very interesting letters. Now Ruth, would you please read our first letter?" I would listen intently as I heard about peoples' pain and suffering being witnessed and understood. There was no punch line at the end of the program—no miraculous conversion. When transformation was alluded to, it was described as gained through insight and struggle.

The Narramores' program was an early evangelical attempt to reclaim the scandal of the evangelical mind withdrawn from science and academia. Evangelicalism had construed psychotherapy as that "other" conversion, creating for Christians a binary that was superficially maintained and should never have existed. Psychoanalysis, that Jewish science and secular foe of faith that European church history had prepared for its role as "other," was pleased to be polar opposite to Christian conversion. Thoughtful evangelicals were coming to the realization that if Christ is Lord over all, his present and coming kingdom must be bringing harmony to sectarian-constructed dualisms spawned in this fallen world. The dualism of a Christianity divorced from Judaic belief in God's redemptive plan to transform a fallen world had for too long foreclosed upon ecumenical discourses of hope. The Christian prayer of "Thy Kingdom Come" must dismantle objectifying binaries like supersessionism[1] and recognize all earthly and spiritual dimensions, present and future dimensions, and individual and communal dimensions, so that the suffering God embodied in Christ's resurrection power may become more fully represented in this world.

In this chapter, I will present the story of Cathy, whose sufferings and growth will illustrate a retraditioned understanding of conversion. As I deconstruct the popular view of conversion, I will contextualize its usage in early twentieth-century evangelicalism. In that deconstruction, I will again posit trauma, both societal and personal, as instrumental in the receptivity of the United States to

---

1. Supersessionism is the belief that the Church has replaced Israel in God's redemptive plan, and Judaism is ostensibly cast aside.

dispensational theology and apocalyptic eschatology. In retraditioning the construct of conversion, I will follow the *telos* of God's redemptive program that begins with witness, continues to salvation, and reaches its zenith in conversion.

CATHY: THE PATIENT WHO ALMOST DESTROYED MY DOG, PART I

Cathy was exhilarated when she married Peter. He was a worship leader whose father and grandfather had pastored his country church. She had now "moved beyond" her less than stellar beginning, though truth be known, she was also intimidated by the Christian pedigree of Peter and his family. Cathy was born in a small Pennsylvania town to parents whose family history held many secrets. Suicides and untimely deaths dotted the genogram, but Cathy knew little of the family history. Nonetheless, she was a bright and ambitious woman, and she rose within the ranks of her Christian community, becoming a leader as well and bringing many young women to faith in Christ through her youth work.

Life moved along well for Cathy until the day she received news that her eighteen-year-old nephew had committed suicide. The chaos of her childhood, the mixture of sadness and rage at her nephew's father—her brother—the feelings of unbearable inferiority to her husband's family, all came crashing in upon the pleasant, bucolic life that she had enjoyed. When she came to see me, her moods were cycling from despair to rage, and she feared her own destructiveness. Once, when angry at her husband, she had taken a pair of scissors and cut to pieces several pairs of his pants. On another occasion, in an explosive rage, she rammed her car into the parked car he occupied. In sessions, she would vacillate from rageful woman to panic-stricken child. It would take true perseverance on her part and mine to allow a witnessing of the many fractals of her childhood sufferings that gave rise to these impulsive, pain-induced, hostile actions.

71

DECONSTRUCTING CONVERSION

The term *conversion* has suffered from considerable ambiguity and slippage in evangelical discourse. Most often, it is used synonymously with *salvation*, though it can also refer to salvation along with a path of reformation that follows it. As camp-meeting evangelism grew under the preaching of Dwight L. Moody and Billy Sunday, American-style, action-based, dispensational theology sculpted "conversion" as an experience made on the basis of a decision for Christ. Billy Sunday's words clearly endorse this version of the word's meaning:

> What does converted mean? It means completely changed. Converted is not synonymous with reformed. Reforms are from without—conversion from within. Conversion is a complete surrender to Jesus. . . . I want you to see what God put in black and white; that there can be a sound, thorough conversion in an instant. . . . What I want and preach is the fact that a man can be converted without any fuss. . . . Matthew stood in the presence of Christ and he realized what it would be to be without Christ, to be without hope, and it brought him to a quick decision. "And he arose and followed him." How long did that conversion take? . . . You can be converted just as quickly as Matthew was. God says: "Let the wicked man forsake his way." The instant that is done, no matter if the man has been a life-long sinner, he is safe. There is no need of struggling for hours—or for days—do it now. . . . "Let the wicked man forsake his way." When? . . . Now! The instant you yield, God's plan of salvation is thrown into gear. You will be saved before you know it, like a child being born.[2]

In Billy Sunday's sermon can be heard a trauma-based emphasis of splitting into black and white, good and evil. The focus on simplicity is also evidence of trauma that dismisses complexity. The denial of complexity correlates with a traumatized person's denial, dismissal, repression, and dissociation of his or her own

---

2. Lawrence, *Greatest Sermons*, 166–71.

trauma. The burgeoning "revivalism" of the nineteenth century was forged through an amalgam of theological influences that, according to George Marsden, also provided " . . . new channels for emphasis on emotion"[3] along with a call to "true" conversion, reflected in Christian holiness. Sizer asserts that centuries-old "social religious meetings," like prayer meetings and Bible studies, were the forerunners to the rise of these massive, emotionally-charged evangelistic meetings[4] where, fueled by catastrophic, apocalyptic urgency, sinners were implored to convert to Christ.

Socio-Cultural Trauma and Conversion

While premillennial eschatologies had previously enjoyed a modest presence in the Christian church, the dispensational rendition of premillenialism spread like wildfire among evangelicals who had been prepared by tumultuous historical events to embrace a theology fraught with dualism. Darby's ideas were fueled by personal and European disillusionments. But trauma as a result of civil war in the United States made it ripe for a shift to pessimism:

> "We had flattered ourselves" wrote an editor during the Civil War . . . "that we should escape the desolating wars which have marked the fluctuating fortunes of European Empire, and that in a pathway of unbroken peace we should sweep forward into the cloudless splendors of the Millenial era."[5]

The ominous onset of the American Civil War fanned doubts in the minds of believers concerning the viability of postmillenial progress. As the Civil War raged on to claim over a million military and civilian lives, this catastrophic national trauma left a parched land prepared for saturation by an eschatology that could make

---

3. Marsden, *Fundamentalism*, 45.

4. Ibid., 5.

5. Moorhead, "Between Progress and Apocalypse," 535.

meaning of omnipresent desolation.[6] World War I only intensified the momentum of a shift toward a pessimistic eschatology.

Concurrent with the trauma of these shattering world events were the developments made in the disciplines of science. The burgeoning interest in Darwin's theories was confirmation to many Christian believers that the Christian nations were not, in fact, ushering in God's golden age.

Personal Trauma and Conversion

In addition to the societal trauma in the United States, there were personal traumatic events that had wounded those who popularized the new dualistic eschatology that was part of the larger dispensational *oeuvre*. Having identified trauma as a precipitating factor in Darby's life, I will recount traumatic events in the lives of those who popularized his teachings in the United States.

James H. Brookes

James Brookes was central to the development of American evangelicalism, principally in his mentoring of C. I. Scofield, but also in his leadership of the Niagara Conference, a prophesy conference that promoted premillennial thought. James was three years old when his father, a Presbyterian minister, suddenly died of cholera. Mother was left in dire circumstances, and when James was eight, she sent him off to live with another family about a hundred miles away, who agreed to house him in return for his labor on their property.

James Brookes's biography begins:

> This is the plain record of the life and works of one who was a fatherless boy, earning his food and garret bed when eight years old; of a needy youth who secured his college education "by the sweat of his brow," and who

---

6. Mangum, "High Hopes," 3.

lived at times, literally, on bread and water while a student . . .[7]

Brookes's diary entry of February 27, 1849 records:

> The history of our family has been a strange one. . . . Father was cut off in the vigor of life. . . . Then my brother, just in the act of attaining the object of his hopes . . . to follow in the footsteps of father in proclaiming God's will to man.
>
> Mother's life has been a continued scene of trials and sorrow. And time, instead of smoothing her pathway to the grave, has only heaped higher the troubles before her but "whom the Lord loveth, He chasteneth." He intends putting our faith to the test, trying its strength on the fierce conflicts, that the path to glory shall not be strewn with flowers.[8]

Brookes enrolled in Princeton Theological Seminary and was ordained to ministry in St. Louis, Missouri at the 16th and Walnut Avenue Presbyterian Church. Following John Darby's visit in 1872, Dr. Brookes became a stalwart supporter of Darby, his church becoming the prominent center of dispensational theology in the United States. Many today, however, consider Brookes' greatest achievement as becoming the mentor of C. I. Scofield. In the following paragraphs, a sampling of Brookes' written sentiments both demonstrate his affinity with Darby's demeanor and theology, and belie his unresolved personal trauma.

BROOKES ON SELF-ESTEEM

> He did not look out on life . . . in the bland manner of the typical young scholastic who goes direct from his seven years of book study into his pulpit. . . . Dr. Brookes had studied men first, and theology afterwards. And it might be said, in passing, that no one ever heard him deliver a

7. Williams, *James H. Brookes*, 9.

8. Ibid., 24–25.

"discourse" on the "nobility of man." His firm belief was that man was "a poor critter," to use the homely phrase.

One day, in later life, a learned guest asked Dr. Brookes if he did not think that "'self-esteem was a most noble attribute of the human mind?"

"Do you really want to know what I think of self-esteem, and of man?" responded Dr. Brookes.

"Yes."

"Well, I'll tell you. I think man ought to have a third leg, to kick himself over Creation with."[9]

Brookes on "Manliness"

Friday noon, —This, to me, is one of the saddest days imaginable. In the distance is just visible my birth-place, the home of my joyous childhood, over which so many sad, most sad changes have come. But I should cast the feeling off. It is not manly." Manliness was his keynote throughout life.[10]

At Northfield, at Geneva, or wherever he was, he was always a lion among the young men. He was so manly, so vigorous, such a hard-hitter at men and things he held to be wrong . . .[11]

Brookes on Sadness and Pessimism

June 8. Sixteen years ago to-day my father died. Though I have no recollection of him, I . . . have often deeply regretted that memory would not bring up the faintest look or action of his."[12]

9. Williams, *James H. Brookes*, 62.

10. Ibid., 30.

11. Ibid.

12. Ibid.

> January 14. To-day I again began my life of labor. Ah!
> mostly it is a toilsome, sad life to me, but for all that it is
> a strengthening, pleasant, toilsomeness, a sweet sadness
> . . .[13]

Cyrus Ingerson Scofield

Cyrus Ingerson Scofield was three months old when, in 1843, his mother died as a result of complications from his birth. Scofield describes a childhood of loneliness, his father largely absent working to support his five children and his four older sisters "shamefully neglecting him."[14] Scofield once ran away from home when quite young. At seventeen, Scofield enlisted in the Confederate Army and fought in the battle of Antietam. In young adulthood, he abused alcohol, abandoned his wife and children, and was convicted of felonies for which he served prison time.

Scofield experienced a dramatic conversion in 1879, and by 1880, he was already catapulted to a prominent role supporting Moody's evangelistic meetings. With no formal theological preparation, Scofield was ordained to preach in 1881. A newspaper article in the *Atchison Daily Patriot* dated August 26, 1881 and picked up by the Topeka, Kansas *Daily Capital* on August 27, 1881 offers a little-known and darker picture of C. I. Scofield:

> Cyrus I. Scofield, formerly of Kansas, late lawyer, politician and shyster generally, has come to the surface again, and promises once more to gather around himself that halo of notoriety that has made him so prominent in the past. . . . Within the past year . . . Cyrus committed a series of St. Louis forgeries that could not be settled so easily, and the erratic young gentleman was compelled to linger in the St. Louis jail for a period of six months.
>
> Among the many malicious acts that characterized his career, was one peculiarly atrocious that has come under our personal notice. Shortly after he left Kansas

13. Ibid., 33.
14. Trumbull, *Life Story of C. I. Scofield*.

... he wrote his wife that he could invest some $1,300 of her mother's money, all she had, in a manner that would return big interest. After some correspondence he forwarded them a mortgage, signed and executed by one Chas. Best, purporting to convey valuable property in St. Louis. Upon this the money was sent to him. Afterwards the mortgages were found to be base forgeries, no such person as Charles Best being in existence, and the property conveyed in the mortgage fictitious . . .

In the latter part of his confinement, Scofield, under the administration of certain influences, became converted, or professedly so . . . the next we hear of him he is ordained as a minister of the Congregational Church, and under the chaperonage of Rev. Goodell, one of the most celebrated divines of St. Louis . . .

A representative of the *Patriot* met Mrs. Scofield (sic) today. . . . As to supporting herself and the children, he has done nothing, said the little woman. . . . I will gladly give him the matrimonial liberty he desires. I care not who he marries, or when, but I do want him to aid me in giving our little daughters the support and education they should have.[15]

In spite of his felonies, lack of theological education, and the reality of no timeframe for spiritual maturation, Scofield spearheaded the Bible school movement, founding, among several other institutions, Philadelphia College of Bible and mentoring Lewis Sperry Chafer.[16]

Categorical Divisions throughout His Interpretation of Scripture

As one of Darby's theological progeny, Scofield espoused a theology of fragmentation of salvific history into rigid, discontinuous periods. This theology that privileges splitting over harmony, is a trauma-generated interpretation that understands scripture in

15. Canfield, *Incredible Scofield*, 79–80.

16. Trumbull, *Life Story of C. I. Scofield*; Canfield, *Incredible Scofield*.

a similar way to how a traumatized person experiences life. The title of his most well-known tract is "Rightly Dividing the Word of God." Scofield divided history into seven dispensations, believing that, "each of the dispensations may be regarded as a new test for the natural man, and each ends in judgment marking his utter failure in every dispensation."[17] Scofield dichotomized law and grace:

> The most obvious and striking division of the Word of truth is that between law and grace. Indeed, these contrasting principles characterize the two most important dispensations: the Jewish and Christian. "For the law was given by Moses, but grace and truth came by Jesus Christ" (John 1:17)...
>
> It is, however, of the most vital moment to observe that Scripture never, in any dispensation, mingles these two principles.... Everywhere the Scriptures present law and grace in sharply contrasted spheres.[18]

Scofield Dichotomized the Post Civil War United States

Thirty-nine years following the end of the civil war, Scofield idealized life in the ante-bellum South, and by implication, devalued other expressions of American culture.

> Rev. Scofield addressed [Confederate Veterans] Camp Sterling Price [Texas] on November 23, 1903.
>
> Using typical Lost Cause rhetoric to encourage the Dallas veterans to feel honorable and spiritual about their battlefield experience... Rev. Scofield reminded his audience that the Confederate movement was the movement of a "religious people" exemplified by the spiritual nature of its leaders like General Lee, General Jackson, and President Davis...
>
> Though defeated militarily, Rev. Scofield preached the "ecstatic adoration" of the Confederate leaders as

17. Scofield, *Rightly Dividing*, 25.
18. Ibid., 55–56.

model men to a virtuous society. . . . Praising the virtues
of the old leaders, Scofield declared, "the life of such men
as Lee and Washington, Stonewall Jackson, and Johnston
is the proof of the purity and propriety of the old regime
and the social conditions of the time before the war."[19]

SCOFIELD DICHOTOMIZED HIS OWN FAMILY

In September 1909, Scofield confided to his daughter Helen
Scofield Barlow:

> [W]ork calls and even louder the call of a purse which
> has grown dismally empty— Scofielditis you know. I hate
> to gather my books and papers for so many flittings as I
> seem doomed to make. When I get rich I am going to
> have 3 homes—one in a winter apartment on Washing-
> ton Heights, NY City, one at Crestwood, one at Sorrento,
> Italy. I shall then have duplicates—triplicates—of every-
> thing in the way of belongings which I especially value—
> works of reference for serious studies; my favorite books,
> prints, etc. I shall live in NY Nov.-February; Sorrento,
> March–May, Crestwood, June-October . . . have courage
> my dear. If my ___itis is ever healed you shall have ease
> too.
>
>   Your loving father.[20]

Though Scofield omitted his daughters from his 1920
biography,

> Abbie Scofield Kellogg and Helen Scofield Barlow con-
> tinued to correspond with their long-absent father. On
> May 4, 1921, a rather melancholy Cyrus Scofield wrote
> to his oldest daughter Abbie the seemingly apologetic
> words, "despite giving no proof of it I have never lived
> so much in my love for you & Helen . . . as during these
> months of growing infirmity."[21]

19. Rushing, "From Confederate Deserter," 103–4.
20. Ibid., 114.
21. Ibid., 116.

Cyrus Ingerson Scofield died on Sunday, July 24, 1921 never having publically acknowledged his two daughters. Helen Scofield Barlow requested a copy of her father's Last Will and Testament and found her name missing. Scofield had prepared his Last Will and Testament in September 1909, the very same month in which he affirmed his love for his daughters and promised to leave to them an inheritance. He, however, made no mention of either Abigail or Helen in that document, but left his entire estate, including significant royalty payments for the Scofield Annotated Bible, to his wife Hettie Scofield and his son, Noel Paul Scofield.[22] This was a particularly egregious example of Scofield separating even his own children into worthy and unworthy, blessed and disowned, good and bad.

Dwight L. Moody

Dwight Moody was four when his father suddenly died in 1841. His family was left destitute. In adulthood, he began Christian ministry with the YMCA, caring for disabled Union soldiers. He made Chicago his permanent home, assumed a pastorate there, and eventually invited John Darby to speak at his church. He affiliated with the Plymouth Brethren, only to later be excommunicated by Darby.[23]

Moody speaks of the impact of the his father's loss and of the subsequent conditions of his family in this sermon excerpt:

> Before I was fourteen years old the first thing I remember was the death of my father [when I was 4]. He had been failed in business, and soon after his death the creditors came in and took everything. My mother was left with a large family of children. One calamity after another swept over the entire household. Twins were added to the family, and my mother fell ill . . . My mother turned to [my older brother] for strength in her calamity. But

22. Ibid., 116–17.
23. Moody, *Life of Dwight L. Moody.*

my brother believed that he must leave home to make a fortune. Away he went and became a wanderer.

Some nights . . . my mother [wept] for my brother who had treated her so unkindly. I used to think she loved him more than all the rest of us put together, and I believe she did.[24]

William Ashley "Billy" Sunday

"Billy" Sunday was five weeks old when his father died in 1862, presumably in a battle as a Union soldier in the Civil War. At the age of ten, Sunday's mother sent him and his brother to a Soldiers' Orphans home. He wrote:

My father went to the war four months before I was born, in Company E, Twenty-third Iowa. I have butted and fought and struggled since I was six years old. . . . I know all about the dark and seamy side of life, and if ever a man fought hard, I have fought hard for everything I have ever gained.

I went back to the old farm some years ago. The scenes had changed about the place. Faces I had known and loved had long since turned to dust . . . I stood and thought. The man became a child again . . .

"Backward, turn backward,

O time in thy flight,

Make me a child again, just for tonight,

Mother, come back from that echoless shore,

Take me again to your heart as of yore.

Into the old cradle I'm longing to creep,

Rock me to sleep, mother, rock me to sleep."[25]

24. Moody, "Mother Moody's Prodigal Son."

25. Ellis, *Billy Sunday*, 27.

Dualism and Conversion

The impingements of personal and geopolitical traumas contributed substantially to the rise of dualistic, pessimistic, dispensational theology and praxis. Conversion became focused upon one's attainment of heaven, and one's passion for evangelism and rejection of materialism in many of its manifestations gave proof to one's attainment of conversion. Thus the emphasis shifted to one's future salvation and spiritual destiny.

Conversion also became a very individual occurrence. While there was acknowledgment that conversion changed one's dealings with one's neighbor, the primary focus was not conversion in order to love better and bring about God's kingdom here and now, but conversion unto the calling of individual holiness and the "winning of souls" in anticipation of the rewards of a future glory. The dualisms of present and future, material and spiritual, and individual and communal cast their shadows upon a diminished understanding of conversion.

While dramatic changes may appear to spontaneously occur at times, and miracles of God are not beyond possibility, I believe there are ample reasons for concern about radical conversions based on decisionism. In such a transaction, a person's past can be put "under the blood," and through "deliverance" such persons are instantaneously accepted as capable of living lives radically detached from previous patterns of living.

Most often, change comes through struggle and travail and progressive surrender to Jesus' loving example. The rush to "victorious living"—a "hopscotch" to resurrection power that skips over suffering—is most clearly observed in the life history of C. I. Scofield, who was catapulted to Christian leadership, and whose checkered past has been sanitized and sequestered from the view of most evangelicals.

Ullman, in an empirical study of conversion, found that dramatic religious conversions such as Scofield's, "occur against a background of emotional turmoil and instability,"[26] with the

26. Ullman, *Transformed Self*, 20.

highest incidence of disruption occurring among individuals who experienced trauma in relationships with their fathers. It is striking that each of these men who introduced dispensational thought to the United States lost their fathers in early childhood—three to death and one to neglect—and were victims of early trauma. Their formative years were chaotic, unjust, and likely without comfort and consolation for their wounds. It is no wonder that each would turn to a theology that was absolutist and that preached separation and escape.

Belief in quick, radical conversions may also be implicated in repetitive egregious behaviors of some evangelical leaders that have occurred in each generation including the present. Attachments that are neurologically based and psychologically dissociated can give way to the power of God; however, we understand from the Christian Scriptures that struggle over a lifespan is part and parcel of spiritual maturation. Conversion is the traverse of a path fraught with suffering as well as a journey of resurrection power.

RETRADITIONING CONVERSION

Comprehensive examinations of the construct of "conversion" have been undertaken by scholars in philosophy, theology, and general psychology such as William James,[27] Lewis Rambo,[28] Newton Malony,[29] and many others who have extended their work in numerous directions. My focus is upon how suffering is essential and formative both in the understanding and experience of "conversion."

I wish to digress and offer a caveat for my inquiry into the construct of conversion. As a psychoanalyst, I anticipate that distorting projections may be embedded in the theological perspectives of a person with dissociated trauma. In making such an assertion,

27. James, *Varieties of Religious Experience.*

28. Rambo, *Understanding Religious Conversion.*

29. Malony, *Handbook of Religious Conversion.*

I acknowledge the always-present potential of collapsing the dialectic of the earthly and spiritual in the direction of the earthly, and thereby implicating myself in the error that I hope to address. True conversion, while relying in part on volitional aspects of the self, is first generated by the unquantifiable, mysterious work of the Holy Spirit. Even traumatically-motivated, pathology-riddled dramatic conversions can contribute to the furtherance of God's kingdom, in spite of taint by human brokenness and myopic vision.

As a Christian and a psychoanalyst, my view of conversion is first informed by God's desire to enter into human suffering and redeem it. As followers of Jesus step into the sufferings of another with resurrection hope, we embody Christ's prayer, "Thy Kingdom Come," not just in the future tense, but in the present tense as well, and not only for an individual, but for the body of Christ. Conversion pertains to both a present and future hope and an individual and communal transformation. Upon this foundational understanding, I would like to address three simultaneous aspects of Christian conversion: as a redemptive process, as a relational process, and as a vocational process.

A Redemptive Process

Fairbairn depicts an inner world freighted by attachment to bad relationships that then protectively fracture the self into fragmented parts via dissociation. This internally divided self is the starting point for my understanding of conversion. If internal wholeness devolved into internal fragmentation, then a redemptive perspective would require that conversion is at minimum a return to wholeness.

The word associated with conversion in the Greek New Testament, *epistrepho*, is amplified by its counterpart in the Hebrew Old Testament, *shuv*. Such amplification is readily available through looking at identical passages in Old and New Testaments. Matthew 13:15 is quoted from its source, Isa 6:10. Matthew, citing Isaiah, writes:

> For this people's heart is waxed gross, and their ears are
> dull of hearing, and their eyes they have closed; lest at any
> time they should see with their eyes, and hear with their
> ears, and should understand with their heart, and should
> be converted [*epistrepho*], and I should heal them.[30]

The original passage in Isaiah reads this way: "Make the heart of
this people fat, and make their ears heavy, and shut their eyes; lest
they see with their eyes, and hear with their ears, and understand
with their heart, and convert [*shuv*], and be healed."[31]

Translation of the Hebrew word *shuv* is most often rendered
"to turn." *Shuv* implies more than just "turning" as in repentance;
it suggests a returning to a previous state or place. In fact, the *New
King James Version* renders *shuv* in Isa 6:10 as "return." Thus, conversion
may be associated with the redemptive return to wholeness,
or at-one-ment implied in Fairbairn's treatment recommendations
for the fragmented self.

A Relational Process

Relational psychoanalysis focuses on the healing of suffering—intrapsychically,
interpersonally, and societally. Its social activism
stems in part from its connection to the historic, subtextual Jewish
vision of the redemption of the world.[32] Following the shattering
events of World War II, Jewish scholars such as Lukacs, Arendt,
Adorno, and Benjamin formed the Frankfurt School. There, according
to Mendieta, "atheistic Jewish Messianism which was very
unique and particular to assimilated central European Jews"[33] robustly
emerged, endeavoring to address issues of the genesis of evil
and the facilitation of social justice. Lukacs, in particular, retained
great influence in his native Budapest, where Sándor Ferenczi, a
progenitor of relational psychoanalysis, practiced.

30. Matt 13:15.

31. Isa 6:10.

32. Aron and Starr, *Psychotherapy for the People*; Greenberg, *For the Sake of Heaven and Earth*.

33. Mendieta, *Frankfurt School on Religion*, 5–6.

More recently, the feminist scholar Jessica Benjamin, who studied at the Frankfurt School, became the leading theoretician for emergent relational psychoanalysis, bringing her work on intersubjectivity and mutual recognition to relational theory.[34] Mutual recognition is central to relational psychoanalytic thought. Through her work, mutual recognition became conceptualized as the capacity to see others as equal subjects, with needs, desires, and perspectives that can differ from one's own, and the reciprocating experience of the other's acknowledgment of one's own subjectivity. Benjamin asserts, along with philosophers including Levinas[35] and Ricoeur,[36] that the capacity to see the other as truly other is fundamental to the achievement of a just society.

While salvation pertains to a release from bondage to bad, internalized relationships and renewed capacity to see aright, conversion progresses toward the return to a state of internal wholeness from which, having right seeing, one is able to conceptualize the "other" as a suffering "other." Conversion opens a space where painful experiences become transformed from "what happened to me" to "what is happening to another." There is a shift from the inward gaze of trauma and loss that is projected out on to the other, to the outward gaze that utilizes past suffering as a resource for being with another as truly other.

A Vocational Process

Conversion is redemptive in its functions within the person and toward other persons, and becomes a process of restoring broken, wounded, and lost parts of a person to a former state of wholeness. Conversion is a relational process in which projections are dismantled and distortions are removed, making possible the experience of knowing another with clear sight, and facilitating reconciliation with God and others. Conversion can be understood as

34. Benjamin, "Recognition and Destruction."

35. Levinas, *Totality and Infinity*.

36. Ricoeur, *Course of Recognition*.

a turning from the idols of broken early attachment figures, and a turning to an undistorted apprehension of God and others.

I recognize in conversion an additional quality or component: that of vocation. In a cycle of eternal return, I find in God's redemptive desires an intention that those whose sufferings have been witnessed and transformed will become witnesses as well. There is first right seeing, which comes with salvation—but sight must proceed to redemptive action. From a Christian and a relational psychoanalytic perspective, projective identification (seeing another through the distortions of one's personal trauma and brokenness) must be converted into empathic identification in which we are able to comfort others through the "comfort wherewith we have been comforted of God."[37] This call to the vocation of being witnesses both to God's resurrection power in our lives and to the suffering of others is predicated upon our having embraced our own suffering. Our suffering—which has been witnessed, acknowledged, comforted, and retrieved out of dissociation and projection[38]—can become transformed into a maturing capability for empathy that may be freely given to comfort others who are suffering.

Conversion, understood in this way, is neither static nor sequential, because in our imperfection, we as helpers repeatedly fall into enactments that objectify the other. Our own old patterns of relating amalgamate with our patients' dynamics, and we fall prey to co-constructing their objectification in our therapeutic relationships against all of our intentions to the contrary. We become sin for our patients, not unlike the One who knew no sin, but most often because of our own projections and the projections of our patients. But we also recognize that God redeems the very substance of our identifications and that they become background to the emerging foreground of our witness to the sufferings in our patient's histories. As we struggle with maintaining our sight, at times we become blinded. When we fail our patients, our repentance and confession to our patients are necessary and can be

37. 2 Cor 1:4.

38. Benjamin, "Identification with the Aggressor."

potentially healing interventions in this conversion process. Relational psychoanalysts refer to this process as "rupture and repair."[39] We oscillate from the immanence of falling prey to an enactment of past wounds to the moment of transcendence, when we recognize our capacity for self-deception and destructiveness. Relying on the witness of our patients and supervisors, our self-reflexivity, and the promptings of the Holy Spirit to alert us to our participation in perpetuating the fragmentation of the other, we follow our own paths of conversion as we repeat again and again the passing from Good Friday to resurrection Sunday—from repentance to celebration.

For the Christian psychotherapist, conversion includes our own refining in which we are always becoming more empathically attuned to each patient. While each person's suffering is unique, our eyes peer in faith toward a shared destiny for all, a destiny that progressively converts human suffering into human witnessing, and the hoped for at-one-ment of salvation. Both our archeological witnessing and our teleological hoping rely on the power of resurrection to redeem the past. The patient's narrative derives new meaning through the redemptive process of psychotherapy, which directs resurrection light back onto a history of suffering. Devin Singh offers us further reflection regarding the transformation of narratives through the resurrection:

> The possibility opened up through the resurrection is the future of history. . . . As a historian discovers hope in the mode of memory, so the prophet shapes memory in the mode of hope. Our past and present must be viewed in light of the future. . . . The resurrection as metaphor has a surplus of meaning. It is a poetic redescription of reality, projecting new possibilities for existence.[40]

Such was the case for the Huguenots who settled in Chambon-sur-Lignon, France, a remarkable example of the conversion of suffering into empathic identification. The inhabitants of this small village in south central France had settled their land in the

---

39. Aron and Mitchell, *Relational Psychoanalysis*.

40. Singh, "Resurrection," 6.

1500s. A small, Lutheran minority in a Catholic country, the Huguenots were persecuted for three centuries. They were hanged, left to die of starvation, of cold or heat, their only crime being that they were Protestants. But their Christian faith was nurtured within a tightly knit, stable community that offered comfort and support, where suffering was witnessed and responded to. Across generations, the narrative of suffering was kept alive through the pastors, for "behind the Huguenot sermon is the history of a besieged minority trying to keep its moral and religious vitality against adversity."[41] Hymnody also kept the history of solidarity in persecution alive.

Chambon-sur-Lignon would come to occupy a pivotal role in the salvation of nearly five thousand Jews during the Holocaust. Under the guidance of a pastor whose vision was unclouded, who saw each person as made in the image of God, and holding in memory their own suffering, the people of Chambon embraced young and old, professors and peasants who fled from Nazi persecution, offering the love of God that had sustained them through generations of their own pain. There was no dissociation of suffering, but rather its embrace. There was no splitting of earthly and spiritual, nor present and future in this mountain village in France. The present and coming kingdom of God was in the suffering, with its potential for dissociation and projective identification, but was repeatedly converted through the crucible of surrender, into a redemptive, empathic identification.

I am convinced that conversion must be transformed from the clichéd term used lightly to designate a response to an altar call. Conversion can then be seen as the lived experience of Isa 61:3 in which we offer what we have first experienced: "Beauty for ashes, the oil of joy for mourning, the garment of praise for the spirit of heaviness; [so that we and our patients together] might be called trees of righteousness, the planting of the Lord, that he might be glorified."[42]

---

41. Hallie, *Lest Innocent Blood*, 172.
42. Isa 61:3.

CATHY: THE PATIENT WHO ALMOST DESTROYED MY DOG, PART II

As Cathy shared her story, I came to understand that she had felt sporadically and marginally close to her father and very distant from her mother and only brother. Though largely unattended to by her parents, Cathy was never alone, for she could be sure that her brother would be there to torment her, rage at her, and dismiss her. Her brother's abusive patterns became more concrete for Cathy when, following her nephew's suicide, she learned that he had in fact been diagnosed with a serious mental illness.

Cathy's mother had always been an enigma for her. Her mother had been repeatedly admitted to hospitals for one medical reason or another. Piecing the puzzle together, we came to believe that her mother's scores of hospitalizations and months of lying alone on her "sick bed" may have reflected undiagnosed Munchausen's disorder. With this awareness, Cathy began experiencing a flood of memories about her mother's many questionable illnesses. Cathy remembered her childhood terror that she had terribly hurt her mother, and her early despair that she might lose her.

Cathy's active dream life reinforced her badness and destructiveness that she felt lay within herself. One dream portrayed me as a zookeeper; I was asked to care for her pet rats, but I needed to keep them in a very secure cage. Other dreams were filled with bloodshed and mutilated bodies. With her long-buried feelings emerging with intensity and rapidity, Cathy lost most of her identification with the woman she had become at her church—the leader, the soul-winner, and the victorious Christian. She even questioned what her Christianity meant and how real it had actually been for her. During this period, Peter had encouraged her to begin counseling and supported her through her suffering. For this Cathy was grateful, but her anger was also aroused, because once again Peter was the saint and she the sinner. It would take several years for Cathy and Peter to deconstruct how their expression of Christianity, which eschewed recognizing suffering and pain, had left its mark on their marriage.

Over a couple of years of work, Cathy came to understand that her radical shifts from rageful person to needy child were really a function of her longing to be close to her mother, father, and brother. She needed to feel attached and had identified with them. She behaved like the terrifying mother, the neglectful father, and the rageful brother toward herself and others. Sometimes, I ached alongside of her; at other times, to my shame, I experienced annoyance at the repetitiveness of her actions. But further exploration of my shame revealed that this is precisely what she felt when her mother would repeatedly be ill. At other times, my mind would become hyper-focused upon the facts of her narrative, and I would feel deadened to her pain. At those times, I had become the mother that lost touch with her daughter, abandoning her emotionally. When Cathy would react to my distance, I became aware of it, apologizing for the way I had inadvertently failed her. In so doing, Cathy experienced something that had never happened in her family.

As Cathy grasped her identification with her family members and the subsequent dissociation of any negative affect that accompanied her history with them, she understood that she had been "occupied" and that these people were extending their control over her life. She began to feel empowered to be who she truly wanted to be. I utilized her Christian terminology to explain that what felt comfortable and familiar was the "natural man." Simultaneously, she was a "new creation"—the person who so lovingly reared her children, did not neglect them, rage at them, or terrify them. Cathy came to understand that she could be that "new creation" person to herself as well. I often utilize Christian terminology when working with evangelicals, and invest the words with new or expanded meanings.

In time, Cathy no longer experienced impulsive outbursts, and when she did, she was able to self-regulate in a brief period of time. But the continued sense that she was bad and sick and dangerous—a clear outworking of her moral defense—would unexpectedly continue to surface. The sins of her family, the memories of her destructive rages, the emotional disturbances in her mother and brother, as well as the suicides—these confirmed for Cathy that in fact, she was not only bad, but also dangerously bad. And now, my dog story.

Rudy, as we call him, came to us when just a few months old, following the death of another beloved Pomeranian. He was an instant hit. He was cute as a button, but his brain cells just had not fully developed yet. Cathy always brought treats for my dogs—she loved my dogs, and they loved her. On an ordinary day, she came in and gave the little treat to Rudy. We went on with our session until she commented to me that Rudy had not moved in a while. I looked down and, to my horror, Rudy was not breathing. I don't know how long he had been in this state, but it was long enough that he involuntarily defecated. I screamed, "My dog is dead, my dog is dead!" as I ran to him, held him upside down and performed the Heimlich to no avail. His lifeless body did not respond. Finally, I laid him on the floor and did CPR—compressions, breaths—as my terror-stricken patient watched. I cleared his airway by hand, and found a treat lodged sideways. But still, no respiration. I tried a second course of CPR. Still nothing. I was giving up hope, but Cathy, who had begun studies in medicine years before, pleaded, "try one more time." I did so, and Rudy began to cough. He was very disoriented, but so were we. He curled up on my lap and slept as Cathy and I talked of what had just happened. How do you go on in a session after something like this?

My mind went quickly to what must have been stirring in Cathy. I asked her what she felt, and we discovered that this incident led to the heart of her fears: Her love and her hate were destructive. She had nearly killed my dog. This led us into explorations of her feelings of responsibility for her mother's well-being, which could oscillate to a virulent hatred for mother's total self-absorption. We discussed her feelings of envy for her brother who had been favored and her guilt over her wishing him ill. Through our shared horror for Rudy's apparent demise, I had not only witnessed Cathy's manifest pain, but I had experienced the terror that she felt about the evil in herself. Until Cathy's dissociated affect spontaneously emerged, these feelings had been unavailable for her to recollect or acknowledge, and we had been unable to access what had perpetually held her in bondage. When Cathy experienced my humanness, my panic, she was able to relinquish her idealization of me and be reassured that her own intense feelings were normative.

Cathy's desire to feel normal and good became more often realized, and she was further freed from the repetitive cycles of anger that reinforced her bad identifications, but she would still have to wait some time for evidences of conversion to empathic identifications.

The first evidence occurred when she decided to return to school and complete her medical training. Although she was in midlife, the earlier constraints of parents who did not encourage her academically were now diminished. Cathy excelled in her studies. Concurrently, she worked in a medical setting in which she experienced deep compassion for suffering people. She had longed to heal her mother and could not; she had longed to be comforted and was not. Now, as an adult, she could offer to herself and others what was denied her in childhood.

The more surprising evidence of conversion emerged not in her career, but in her marriage. A previously undisclosed revelation by Peter of a long-buried falsehood enraged Cathy. She had been the trusting, defective wife, while Peter had been the saint, and it had all been a lie. Her rage returned with a vengeance, and some of Cathy's maturational gains were eclipsed, at least for a time.

In a reversal that Benjamin refers to as a "doer-done to" complementarity,[43] Cathy, who had been the victim in a patriarchal system, experienced a reversal in the direction of her intrapsychic dynamic, and her enacted rage was doing to Peter what had been done to her. For months, Cathy remained regressed and distant from Peter for whom she felt unbaiting rage, until a space opened in which she could mourn. Only after Cathy's illusions of Peter's perfection and her defectiveness were laid bare could she see her role in maintaining Peter's defenses against knowing his

43. Benjamin, "Beyond Doer and Done To."

own suffering and recognizing both his own neediness and his own evil. Cathy began to see that Peter's family, who had appeared spotless, was riddled with falsehood and unacknowledged pain. After a significant period of her reactive disdain of Peter and his family, Cathy gingerly moved toward empathy for her husband, who she could eventually understand as someone who suffered from his own unrecognized and unacknowledged psychic pain, just like she had. After this reparative period in her marriage, old feelings of defectiveness projected on to her by her parents and brother only rarely threatened her, and she could experience empathic identification with Peter, who could now acknowledge his own suffering. Peter is in his own psychotherapy, and together they have come to see themselves as broken and wondrous, enjoying their marriage more than they ever had thought possible.

CONCLUSION

I conclude this focus on conversion with a note that Cathy gave me, sharing her feelings of disbelief and wonder at the growth that has occurred in her life. She wrote:

> Projectors are artists. They make an art of drawing portraits of themselves on your soul. Their blackness, their shame, their emptiness, their evil. When you've been trained as a child to allow them to paint their portrait over yours, you become confused. In your heart, you know the ugly picture they've painted doesn't look like you. But you begin to doubt yourself. It hurts, deeply. Sometimes you know the portrait they've painted looks familiar, but you're not sure why, because you're focused on the hurt you feel and the urgent desire to defend yourself. If only you can step out of yourself, turn and look yourself in the face, you would instantly see the transparent portrait of the projector layered over your own face.
>
> The psychologist teaches you what has happened, and it's like standing in front of a portrait at the art museum, studying it, captivated by it. And then you recognize the distortion for what it is: an obliteration of the goodness

of your heart, reflected in the distorted face. When you've learned to identify the projector and the unique feeling when he paints his face over yours, you become free to peel off the offending layer. And you begin to see the real person you are. And you want to cry, because you weren't allowed to see it before. It's good, just like you knew it was . . .

5

FURTHER REFLECTIONS
Redeeming the Consequences

The lens through which I am studying American evangelical personal and cultural histories is trauma. I acknowledge that other cogent analyses may propound alternate meanings.

When trauma becomes dissociated because of its painful nature, it manifests as splits within individual personalities and also in the ideas those traumatized people put forth. I will now examine and offer commentary on three over-arching splits that inhered from the teachings of nineteenth- and twentieth-century dispensational theologians and evangelists, and that profoundly impacted the evangelical Christians' view of and action in culture: A horizontal split, a vertical split, and a temporal split. I will then offer cursory considerations for restoration of a fractured evangelicalism by a return to the ancient narrative of redemption that commences with incarnation, suffers crucifixion, and resolves through resurrection. I hope and pray for visionaries who will expand and implement these cursory considerations.

THE HORIZONTAL SPLIT: EVANGELICAL NEO-PLATONISM

Evangelicalism's separation from culture produced a split between the sacred and secular, between one embedded in society and another separated from it, with disastrous personal and societal consequences. Vic Reasoner summarizes evangelical neo-Platonism:

> George Marsden wrote that between 1900–1930 there was a "great reversal" among American evangelicals . . . toward premillennialism. Marsden demonstrates that the influence of dispensationalism upon the nineteenth century holiness movement shifted personal sanctification from the ethical to the experiential. Sanctification became something mystical and passive which tended to reduce Christian involvement in political activities. According to Rodney Reed, by 1930 the holiness churches had abandoned most of their social concerns . . .
>
> In 1878 William E. Blackstone wrote that premillennialism "gives us a view of the world, as a wrecked vessel, and stimulates us to work with all our might to save some." C. I. Scofield declared that not one of the Apostles was a reformer. Joseph Seiss declared, "The Gospel, as now preached, is not, and in the present order of things never will be, triumphant . . ." Dwight L. Moody declar[ed] that he looked at the world as a wrecked vessel and comment[ed] on evangelicalism's social irrelevance . . .[1]

This horizontal split at the personal level culminated in a narcissistic, inner-focused, mystical experience of personal sanctification that insulates believers from the "evils" of the world until death or rapture. At the ecclesiastic level, evangelicalism separated from "the social gospel," seeing it as a perversion of the "true gospel" that "saves" sinners from hell.

---

1. Reasoner, "Hope of a Christian World," 1–2.

Healing the Horizontal Split: Incarnation, Identification, Witnessing

Untold suffering of evangelical Christians went unwitnessed for generations and was denied transformation through a relational experience of resurrection power. This is in part due to a truncated view of witnessing that convinced believers to deny their suffering because it impeded the church's mission of "saving lost sinners from hell."[2]

Evangelical attempts to become incarnational are underway. Stephen Ministers, lay counselors, support groups, and church-sponsored programs are attempts to turn the tide of unacknowledged human suffering. Pastoral counseling—which was rejected by early twentieth-century evangelical churches as part of the feminized "social gospel"—is reappearing in the evangelical church. The number of available Christian counselors has swelled; programs geared toward training lay and professional counselors matriculate thousands of helpers on a yearly basis.

Concurrently, we have seen an alarming increase of reported scandals in evangelical churches ranging from fraud to prostitution, child sexual abuse, and hidden affairs. These scandals have sullied the ministries of many such as Jim Bakker, Jimmy Swaggart, Paul Cain, Ted Haggard, Bill Gothard, Jack Hyles, and Bob Jones University. Evidence is mounting of child sexual abuse that has gone unreported in evangelical churches. Boz Tchividjian, former chief prosecutor in the Seventh Judicial Circuit's Sexual Crimes Division and professor of law, recounts his experience during the recent Sovereign Grace Ministries sexual abuse scandal that was allegedly covered up. He writes,

> Do we not learn from the past at all? . . . It's been a disappointment probably more than anything else . . . knowing that there are many, many hurting Christians out there, survivors of abuse who are left completely abandoned in many ways by the evangelical community.[3]

2. Makant, "Re-membering Redemption."

3. Tchividjian, "Evangelical Sex Abuse Record."

In 2013, Tchividjian initiated an online petition through GRACE ministries "decrying the 'silence' and 'inattention' of evangelical leaders to sexual abuse in their churches."[4] Tchividjian believes that scandals that will emerge from Protestant churches will make the Catholic sexual scandals pale in comparison.

Hidden moral failures abound in the evangelical church. Several years ago, our family stayed at a large resort and convention center in the western United States. We befriended the general manager, who related that his resort had recently hosted a national gathering of evangelical pastors. To our dismay, he shared with ashen face that the highest volume of in-room, X-rated movie purchases in the history of the resort occurred during this evangelical pastors' conference.

The question begs to be asked: "How can such behavior flourish in the evangelical church?" One plausible though disturbing answer is that such widespread abuse has always existed in evangelicalism. I believe that the very trauma contained in the still influential teaching of the traumatized founders of early evangelicalism perpetuate the ongoing misery and failings of evangelicals who order their lives around their faulty theology of ignoring present suffering.

A related question might inquire why the benefit of scores of thousands of helping lay and professional counselors seemingly has so little effect. I understand that the preponderance of Christian counseling focuses on what is consciously accessible to both client and counselor, leaving unaddressed the deeper, unconscious traumas that remain dissociated that continue to be acted out and re-enacted repeatedly. More profound trauma cannot be witnessed unless highly skilled helping professionals, trained to work with unconscious dynamics, are available to provide the healing process. Such psychotherapy can only be offered by practitioners who themselves have experienced depth psychotherapy. Tragically, many unwary people are retraumatized by helping professionals who commit boundary violations and offer insufficient care, due to their own insufficient personal insight and limited professional

4. Ibid.

experience and training. A further cause of grave concern is the reality that only a fraction of secular and Christian counselors and psychologists have experienced their own extensive personal psychotherapy. Thus they unwittingly visit upon their clients and patients the very traumas that they unconsciously carry and live out in their personal and professional relationships.

Possibilities

For the church to become a haven for transparency and healing, psychotherapy provided by skilled clinicians could become one of the church's gifts to its people. Three initiatives might achieve this level of care.

First, churches in a given region or denomination may cooperate to establish a clinic staffed with well-trained clinicians who offer a continuum of care for church referrals according to their ability to pay. These clinicians could work with lay caregivers in a congregation who themselves have experienced in-depth psychotherapy. Pioneering initiatives that have led the way in such endeavors include the post-World War II Mennonite Mental Health Services and the post-World War I Tavistock Clinic, dubbed the "Parson's Clinic" for its early staffing by Christian psychoanalysts. Frank Lake's clinical theology project is also a well-known service that establishes depth pastoral counseling in the British church.[5]

Second, a national initiative funded by multiple grants could provide intensive psychotherapy for willing pastors and impaired pastors. This initiative could be combined with a retraining within the pastor's tradition that emphasizes integration and education specific to reconciling dualistic interpretative schemas. Pastors who successfully complete personal therapy could receive ongoing support and certification, which could assist search committees for pastoral searches and installations.

Finally, graduate programs and seminaries can offer specializations in theology and dynamic psychotherapy for use

---

5. Lake, *Clinical Theology*.

in Christian ministry. Currently, Sioux Falls Seminary offers such training in their Doctor of Ministry program in Pastoral Psychoanalysis.

THE VERTICAL SPLIT: CHAUVINISM

Not only was a split between earth and heaven created, but also a split between "us" and "them" on earth, between those who have the "truth" and those who are "apostate," "compromisers," and "without the Lord." A militant gospel that dismissed and sometimes disdained any who would "pollute the truth" became the shibboleth of the American evangelical persona.[6]

What was being dissociated in this move to militancy? Trauma produces an unutterable experience of vulnerability, powerlessness, and need. When loss, death, suffering, and disillusionment are not acknowledged and mourned, corresponding affective states are dissociated, and a manic embrace of strength and certainty strengthens the defense. Dispensational theology privileged such strength and "manliness" and denigrated more maternal attributes. Anna Gavanas describes this augmented splitting of stereotypically maternal and paternal attributes:

> "Muscular Christianity" consisted mainly of a series of publications and revival meetings between 1904 and 1918 led by the preachers Dwight Moody and Billy Sunday. . . . One aim of the muscular Christians was to revirilize the image of Jesus, who they felt had become too feminized with his long hair, thin chest, and flowing gowns. Muscular Christianity redesigned Jesus from, in Billy Sunday's words, an "effeminate," "sissified," "dainty," and "lily-livered" image into a tough and muscular working-class hero [as quoted in Kimmel, 1996, p. 179].[7]

Darby, Brookes, Scofield, Moody, and Sunday each suffered profound loss and trauma and lived a Stoic Christian narrative in which pain, need, and vulnerability were no longer relevant. Their

6. Dueck and Reimer, *Peaceable Psychology.*

7. Gavanas, *Fatherhood Politics,* 109.

focus was on the need of others for salvation and the vulnerability of others to eternal damnation. Their beliefs became a defense against the experience of suffering—a massive, collective group denial that has in subsequent generations become a Christian virtue.

At the ecclesiastic level, dispensational theology dichotomized the world in a paranoid split in which "truth-bearers" were no longer vulnerable sojourners in a suffering and hostile world. Projecting their personal vulnerabilities into a dying world—"a sinking ship"—masculinized evangelicals saw themselves as rescuers. Aggressive "soul-winning" reconfigured the church through a proliferation of marketing techniques, mass media initiatives, and a "can-do" American individualist credo. At the personal level, the eschewal of need and vulnerability within evangelicalism produced alienation in those who were suffering, many of whom found solace in psychotherapy and para-church groups, such as Alcoholics Anonymous. Tragically, many suffering Christians became "casualties" of failing to "fight the good fight of faith," deserters who staggered under the weight of an illusory goal of achieving "victorious Christian living." While such militant Christian living is more muffled in much contemporary evangelical practice, untold numbers of evangelicals do not disclose personal struggles for fear of being perceived as not being worthy of Christian service.

At personal and ecclesiastic levels, dissociated suffering suffused evangelicalism with a sense of powerlessness that was unacknowledged and projected outward on to others. "Christian soldiers" perennially prepared for coming persecutions. The evangelical history of transgenerationally-transmitted, dissociated trauma fostered sexist, chauvinistic superiority and privileged masculinity that denigrated maternal nurture.

Healing the Vertical Split: Crucifixion, Surrender, Salvation

Crucifixion is a surrender to weakness and vulnerability, to suffering and shame, and a relinquishing of omnipotent superiority. Crucifixion within evangelicalism would involve a re-owning of personal weakness projected on to others, a movement only made possible when one's own pain is witnessed and acknowledged.

In Hegel's 1824 lectures, he conceived of God's move toward reconciling the world to himself in crucifixion as an essential moment in that reconciliation process:

> Reconciliation begins with differentiated entities standing opposed to each other [negation]—God, who confronts a world that is estranged from him, and a world that is estranged from its own essence. . . . Reconciliation is the negation of this separation, this division, and means that each cognizes itself in the other, finds itself in its essence [1824 lectures 3:171–72].[8]

At the ecclesiastic level, crucifixion requires an acknowledgment of and surrender to evangelicalism's own neediness. G. K. Chesterton memorialized this necessary surrender in "A Hymn for Church Militant":

> Great God, that bowest sky and star
> Bow down our towering thoughts to Thee,
> And grant us in a faltering war
> The firm feet of humility.
>
> Lord, we that snatch the swords of flame,
> Lord, we that cry about Thy car.
> We too are weak with pride and shame.
> We too are as our foemen are.
>
> Yea, we are mad as they are mad.
> Yea, we are blind as they are blind,
> Yea, we are very sick and sad
> Who bring good news to all mankind.
>
> Lord, when we cry Thee far and near
> And thunder through all lands unknown
> The gospel into every ear
> Lord, let us not forget our own.[9]

---

8. Hodgson, *Hegel and Christian Theology*, 97.

9. Chesterton, *Poems*, 55.

Questioning evangelical, Julie Rodgers, revives Chesterton in her blog entry, "Casualties in the Culture War":

> If we're going to follow the leader of our faith, we have to walk with people . . .
>
> We're stifling the spirits of the silent ones among us: our Sunday school students, friends, classmates—our own children. Perhaps a better response would be to model that of Christ's, whose answer to the human notion of "kill or be killed" was to lose His own life to offer hope to the hurting . . .
>
> I'm not asking for a ceasefire in the culture war because I'm some "Jesus is my homeboy" free lovin' hippy; I say it because our faith is fundamentally a call to follow in Christ's footsteps. . . . Not only do we minister to those "on the other side" in doing so, but we minister to the silent ones in our midst—the ones who feel forced into a flip-flop life of secrecy because they're too ashamed to share. . . . I can't imagine Christ sought to speak soldiers into being when He sat on a mountain and said: Blessed are the meek, blessed are the merciful, blessed are the pure in heart, blessed are the peacemakers. And merciful people are safer than soldiers when a casualty needs a place to heal.[10]

At a personal level, crucifixion can be a vehicle of salvation from bondage to internalized, destructive attachments to injurious early caregivers with whom men and women remain identified to their detriment, and whom they relentlessly remain attached to and in turn project on to unsuspecting others. These early attachments predispose people to doctrinally perpetuated, tenderness-aversive spiritual narratives and practices, which erect walls between oneself and his or her personal suffering that is perennially denied.

The ancient Christian narrative offers a response to the cry of despairing evangelicals who recoil from the triumphalism of a designer-branded, all-knowing church: embrace the suffering that crucifixion entails; recognize the personal need for salvation from bondages persisting within us; hold the dialectic of strength and

10. Rodgers, "Casualties in the Culture War."

vulnerability, good and evil with oneself and others; and offer and receive forgiveness.

Without evangelical chauvinism and its preferencing of "masculine" sensibilities, mystery and vulnerability can re-emerge. In place of aggressiveness and superiority, evangelicals may embrace the vulnerability of maternal nurture and surrender to suffering with people famished for comfort and authentic love.

Salvation: As Ongoing Process

Moving away from a model of salvation that is decision-based, evangelicals can recover an understanding of salvation as the lived experience of becoming free from bondage to internal, destructive attachments (the "sins of one's fathers and mothers," Exodus 20) that are unconsciously enacted in unloving, external perceptions and behaviors toward others. This understanding of salvation is consistent with the Biblical notion of being "slaves to sin." The longing for relational attachment that keeps a person in bondage to early faulty attachments to broken caregivers is not in itself pathological. God created people for relationship. When cultures of mutual vulnerability and loving support flourish in the evangelical church, people can relinquish early degrading attachments to early caregivers in the presence of possibilities for new and healthy relational attachments in Christian community. The calling of all followers of Jesus is to surrender to crucifixion. Factions, divisions, and power structures within the evangelical church can give way as people's incomplete understandings of salvation are dismantled, and each person recognizes their own and others brokenness, vulnerability, and need of grace.

Possibilities

Biblical counselors, such as those trained at the Christian Counseling and Educational Foundation (CCEF), have long seen the church as the most vital nexus of "soul care." Though their methods

often fail to reach the deepest level of suffering, the Biblical counseling movement has rightly seen the necessity of counseling being
embedded in Christian community for church-wide restoration to
take root and grow. Three initiatives by evangelical churches could
contribute to such restorative growth.

First, the creation of foster families within churches can
provide congregants with the care they need. These families can
be supported by clinical staff. No longer will so many single, divorced, widowed, and orphaned people find holidays painful because they are alone. They can develop new attachments within the
church with people who themselves are sufficiently safe and loving
and who foster their own development in fellowship and support
groups. Additionally, foster families can be available to accept
people who must find safe haven during abuse situations, periods
of non-life threatening emotional turmoil, or other situations in
which safe housing is needed. I often experience frustration in my
work with people who desperately need such a place, and find no
home open to them.

Second, evangelical churches can re-establish an intentional
and actively-involved "god-parent" initiative for people who lack
permanent connections to family, and/or sufficient role models for
spiritual formation.

Finally, the church can recover its rich heritage and be a
home for people struggling with serious mental illness. A striking example that has become part of a national movement in
Belgium is the Geel community.[11] Since the thirteenth century,
Geel residents have opened their homes to de-institutionalized
psychiatric patients, who are supervised by hospital clinicians but
live in host homes. This initiative was started through the Catholic
Church and remains a current method of providing compassionate, residential, and effective psychiatric care. Though this model
has been often studied, it has mostly been found too revolutionary
to implement. The evangelical church can bring the kingdom of
God to "the least of these" instead of deferring to state sponsored

11. Schwartz, "Medieval Antecedents."

"group homes" where more severely impaired people are housed apart from loving, church community.

I gratefully want to recognize the many individual family units in the evangelical church who have practiced such love of neighbor. I am also calling evangelical communities to provide the structure and support for families to provide this depth of love in every community.

THE TEMPORAL SPLIT: PRIVILEGING THE FUTURE; MINIMIZING THE PRESENT; DISMISSING THE PAST

The Christian church's once optimistic view of "last days" was to follow Jesus' example to reform the world, one person at a time—to live out and enact in one's daily life "Thy Kingdom come on earth as it is in heaven." The prevailing pessimistic view of "end times" eschews any initiatives to bring heaven to earth and instead encourages believers to somehow plod through life and look forward to heaven. In this myopic forward look, an integration of past riches often becomes lost and is replaced by a unidirectional, linear preoccupation with the world to come.

At the personal level, past, present, and future are split apart by dispensational-derived theologies into discrete disconnected categories in the mind of the believer. A person's traumatic and unloving past is rendered "under the blood." Individual Christians are loath to share ongoing struggles with sin, since the milestone of their conversion is behind, and sin should no longer "have hold" on the person. An example of such splitting is the forgotten, private life of C. I. Scofield.

At the ecclesiastic level, the richness of past traditions, liturgies, and a resplendent history of social justice became irrelevant because of Christ's imminent return. The academy that the church established became forfeited in service of purity. Science and faith "dis-integrated" from a theology that viewed the world as racing toward Armageddon. Literature, culture, the arts, and theater were wasteful indulgences in the end times. Church became an event on a Sunday or Wednesday, scheduled in time, rather than a daily community living together with one another in the world.

Temporal splitting has dismissed a recognition and acceptance of suffering and struggle, proscribing instead an unswerving forward gaze toward future deliverance. This traumatically-constructed linear theology, which splits experience into past, present, and future, fosters dis-integration in personal living and discourages relational comforting and being comforted in community.

Healing the Temporal Split: Resurrection, Gratitude, Conversion

The promise of resurrection gives hope in the midst of suffering. It is the pinnacle of the redemptive process whereby Christ confirms His desire and power to redeem all that was destroyed in the fall. N. T. Wright explains:

> Let us remind ourselves of the starting point. The created order, which God has begun to redeem in the resurrection of Jesus, is a world in which heaven and earth are designed not to be separated but to come together. In that coming together, the "very good" that God spoke over creation at the beginning will be enhanced, not abolished.[12]

God has not abandoned us to survive in this lost cause called Earth! And he desires to bring redemption through our weakness in his grand project to restore creation. Gratitude accompanies the belief in Jesus' resurrection, a first-fruit of God's ultimate salvation, and empowers His followers to co-participate in His redemptive program here on earth.

My recent lexicographic study of the operation of gratitude,[13] based on Ricoeur's methodology, sheds light on gratitude's redemptive action. Implicit in the definition of gratitude is a motivation to

---

12. Wright, *Surprised by Hope*, 259.

13. Hoffman, *Toward Mutual Recognition*.

give forward in some way. Contemporary research elucidates this tendency.

In a study by Bartlett and DeSteno, two groups were asked to participate in a tedious task. One group engaged in a repetitive eye-hand coordination task, which had to be aborted and retaken due to an alleged computer failure. At this point in the experiment, a "benefactor," who was actually a member of the research team, offered to help and was able to solve the computer problem, making it unnecessary to repeat the task. This "gratitude" group was then compared with a neutral, control group who completed the task with no computer difficulty and no benefactor. Members of both groups were then asked both by the benefactor or a complete stranger if they would be willing to help with a difficult task. Participants who experienced the situation that evoked gratitude spent more time helping both benefactor and stranger alike than participants who had not experienced gratitude. The findings demonstrated that pro-social behavior is augmented by gratitude, and that pro-social behavior subsequent to the experience of gratitude exists independently from a motivation to reciprocate.[14] Similarly, Paul Ricoeur found this pro-social behavior in his study of the Maori tribe, where gift-giving practices point to a universal desire to pass on the gift as part of the action of gratitude.[15]

Conversion: For the Christian, For the World

People become grateful to God as they experience his progressive salvation in their lives. The desire to reciprocate out of gratitude empowers and redirects conversion away from what was once destructive, and toward God's loving redemptive program. Such an understanding of conversion conjoins the split between past and present, for it is from the ashes of yesterday that God accomplishes restoration in his redemptive plan for all of his creation.

---

14. Bartlett and DeSteno, "Gratitude and Prosocial Behavior."

15. Ricouer, *Course of Recognition*.

Possibilities

Conversion within the church can occur when a person restored from his or her personal suffering can offer redemptive love to others. Members of the community who are overcoming suffering, trauma, disabling attachments, and related challenges can be wisely prepared to become caregivers. Much like Alcoholics Anonymous sponsorship, people recovering from past suffering can be supported by more mature "converts" with histories of similar wounding, who in turn may be supported by pastoral and clinical caregivers. Divorce recovery, suicide survivors, addiction dependencies, conception and adoption concerns, chronic physical and mental illness, financial mentoring—all offer opportunities for grateful giving forward that converts others' chaos and suffering through redemptive love.

Women and men who are divorced and do not plan to remarry, those who are widowed, or those who have remained single may be invited into sisterhoods and brotherhoods not unlike the Catholic tradition. In these groups, specific callings can emerge which give meaning to the single status and convert the aloneness of that singleness into sources of great good, fulfilling relationships both for the single person and the recipients of their care.

In this final chapter, I have painted with broad strokes. None of my possibility sketching is intended to be prescriptive. Rather, my hope is that each follower of Jesus will, in the context and with the support of missional communities of faith, live out their own expression of Jesus' personal love and care for others while he sojourned with us at the beginning of the Christian era.

6

EPILOGUE

The year 1917 was marked by significant publications in both American evangelicalism and in psychoanalysis. Here in the United States, C. I. Scofield published the first complete version of his annotated *King James Version Bible*. This landmark publication was the first presentation to the mass populace of dispensational theology. That theology was systematized by John Darby who was damaged by trauma and loss; the annotations were written by Scofield, also scarred by unresolved trauma and loss, and the annotated Bible was marketed to a citizenry ravaged by the incalculable trauma and loss of the Civil War and the subsequent world-encompassing cataclysm of World War I. Calamity and imminent apocalypse repopulated the pages of the once glorious gospel of Jesus Christ with otherworldly formulations and dualistic, moralizing categories in footnotes on nearly every page of the Scofield Bible. Death, loss, and suffering could now be mere footnotes as well, for preoccupation with the glorious estate of the redeemed in the bye and bye would anesthetize each present sorrow with heavenly sunlight and joy.

In Vienna, Sigmund Freud was working through the tragedy of World War I himself. He commenced his thinking about mourning and loss in this brief 1915 article, writing:

> We may already derive one consolation from this discussion: our mortification and our painful disillusionment on account of the uncivilized behaviour of our fellow-citizens of the world during this war were unjustified. They were based on an illusion to which we had given way. In reality our fellow-citizens have not sunk so low as we feared, because they had never risen so high as we believed . . .[1]

He concluded by saying:

> Would it not be better to give death the place in reality and in our thoughts which is its due, and to give a little more prominence to the unconscious attitude towards death which we have hitherto so carefully suppressed? This hardly seems an advance to higher achievement, but rather in some respects a backward step—a regression; but it has the advantage of taking the truth more into account, and of making life more tolerable for us once again. To tolerate life remains, after all, the first duty of all living beings. Illusion becomes valueless if it makes this harder for us.[2]

In 1917, Freud would go on to write "Mourning and Melancholia," an essay about the effects of loss that is not mourned, but denied. In a famous excerpt, he wrote, "the shadow of the object fell upon the ego,"[3] by which he meant that the ungrieved loss of a loved one deteriorates into an irrational identification with the one who is gone. Such an identification subsequently emerges as depression or a turn to feverish activities.

Oskar Pfister, both a Swiss Reformed pastor and a psychoanalyst, recognized Freud's profound and relevant perspectives on

---

1. Freud, "Thoughts for the Times," 284.
2. Ibid., 298.
3. Freud, "Mourning and Melancholia," 248.

living truthfully, perspectives that were to become more and more alien to evangelical Christianity. He wrote to Freud:

> Finally you ask why psycho-analysis was not discovered by any of the pious, but by an atheist Jew. The answer obviously is . . . that most of the pious did not have it in them to make such discoveries . . . you are not godless, for he who lives the truth lives in God, and he who strives for the freeing of love "dwelleth in God" (First Epistle of John, iv, 16). If you raised to your consciousness and fully felt your place in the great design, which to me is as necessary as the synthesis of the notes is to a Beethoven symphony, I should say of you: A better Christian there never was . . .[4]

Oskar Pfister advocated for depth psychotherapy within the church and established and promulgated the discipline of pastoral counseling in Europe and the United States. But pastoral counseling was dismissed as irrelevant by a dispensationalism that gripped the United States. And so, depth pastoral counseling became predominantly the domain of "liberal" Christianity, and "one-size-fits-all" proof-texted, "Biblically-based," prescriptive counseling the domain of evangelicalism. Biblically-based, behaviorally-oriented counseling that minimized and marginalized suffering offered struggling evangelicals no choice other than to turn for help to depth psychotherapists outside of the church.

I wish to conclude these thoughts and observations I have shared by offering a vision for the church. The paths that never should have parted in an ante-bellum evangelicalism—intellectual rigor, psychological depth, and fervent faith—are awaiting reunification within numerous expressions and traditions of evangelical faith. As contemporary, secular psychology moves toward the dismissal of suffering through cognitive and behavioral techniques that are more motivated by economic than humanitarian concerns, Evangelicals have an opportunity to recapture what was lost over a century ago. As we recommit ourselves to witness the suffering of the world and of our neighbor, and as we walk out our salvation

4. Pfister, "Letter from Oskar Pfister," 62.

from our enslavement to the destructive relationships of our past, we can convert others' suffering and our own into a font of redemption for a world bereft of love. As a body of believers committed to Christ's prayer, "Thy Kingdom Come," we can restore the church through following Jesus' example of relating to others with compassionate care and love for our neighbors.

Like John Darby, I see the New Jerusalem descending. But I see God's habitation with humans, here, on earth. Jesus surely will wipe away all tears in the *eschaton*—but we, his followers, will have prepared the way for the Son of God by the tears that we wipe now with hope and in faith of that day of final consummation.

BIBLIOGRAPHY

Angelou, Maya. *The Complete Collected Poems of Maya Angelou*. New York: Random, 1994.

Armistead, M. Katherine, Brad Strawn, and Ronald Wright. *Wesleyan Theology and Social Science: The Dance of Practical Divinity and Discovery*. Newcastle-Upon-Tyne, UK: Cambridge Scholars, 2010.

Aron, Lewis, and Stephen A. Mitchell. *Relational Psychoanalysis: The Emergence of a Tradition*. Hillsdale, NJ: Analytic, 1999.

Aron, Lewis, and Karen Starr. *A Psychotherapy for the People: Toward a Progressive Psychoanalysis*. New York: Routledge, 2012.

Bartlett, Monica Y., and David DeSteno. "Gratitude and Prosocial Behavior: Helping When It Costs You." *Psychological Science* 17 (2006) 319–25.

Benjamin, Jessica. "Beyond Doer and Done To: An Intersubjective View of Thirdness." *Psychoanalytic Quarterly* 73 (2004) 5–46.

———. "Identification with the Aggressor and the Failed Witness." Presentation at IPTAR, New York, NY, 2011.

———. "Recognition and Destruction: An Outline of Intersubjectivity." In *Relational Psychoanalysis: The Emergence of a Tradition*, edited by Lewis Aron, and Stephen A. Mitchell, 181–210. Hillsdale, NJ: Analytic, 1990.

Birtles, Elinor F., and David E. Scharff. *From Instinct to Self: Selected Papers of W. R. D. Fairbairn, Volume II: Applications and Early Contributions*. Northvale, NJ: Jason Aronson, 1994.

Bonar, Horatius. *Trinity Hymnal*. Reprint, 1861. Suwanee, GA: Great Commission, 1961.

Bonhoeffer, Dietrich. *Meditations on the Cross*. London: John Knox Westminster, 1998.

Boulanger, Ghislaine. *Wounded by Reality: Understanding and Treating Adult Onset Trauma*. New York: Routledge, 2007.

Bromberg, Philip M. "Something Wicked This Way Comes: Trauma, Dissociation, and Conflict: The Space Where Psychoanalysis, Cognitive Science, and Neuroscience Overlap." *Psychoanalytic Psychology* 20 (2003) 558–74.

Brown, Warren, and Brad Strawn. *The Physical Nature of Christian Life: Neuroscience, Psychology, and the Church.* New York: Cambridge University Press, 2012.

Canfield, Joseph M. *The Incredible Scofield and His Book.* Eugene, OR: Ross, 1988.

Cassel, Elijah. *50 Uncommon Songs: For Partakers of the Common Salvation.* Reprint, 1902. Jefferson, OR: Timeless Truths, 2014.

Castiello, Umberto, et al. "Wired to Be Social: The Ontogeny of Human Interaction." *PLoS ONE* 5.10 (2010).

Chalmers, Thomas. *The Expulsive Power of a New Affection.* Reprint, 1855. Minneapolis, MN: Curiosmith, 2012.

Chesterton, Gilbert K. *Poems by G. K. Chesterton.* Claremont, CA: Pomona, 2014.

Costello, John E. *John Macmurray: A Biography.* Edinburgh, UK: Floris, 2002.

Darby, John Nelson. "Affliction's Lessons." *Stem Publishing.* Online: http://www.stempublishing.com/authors/darby/PRACTICE/16054E.html

———. "Christ for My Sins; and Christ for My Cares." *Stem Publishing.* Online: http://www.stempublishing.com/authors/darby/MISCELLA/34018E.html

———. "The Effect of Christ Down Here." *Stem Publishing.* Online: http://www.stempublishing.com/authors/darby/EXPOSIT/27021E.html

———. "The Effect of Christ in Glory." *Stem Publishing.* Online: http://www.stempublishing.com/authors/darbyPOSIT/27022E.html

———. "The Irrationalism of Infidelity: Being a Reply to 'Phases of Faith.'" *Stem Publishing.* Online: http://www.stempublishing.com/authors/darby/APOLOGY/06000E.html

———. *Letters of J. N. D., Vol. I–III.* Sunbury, PA: Believer's Bookshelf, 1971a.

———. "Pilgrim Portions: Week Six." *Stem Publishing.* Online: http://www.stempublishing.com/authors/darby/Pilgrim_Portions.html#a6

———. "Reflections upon the Prophetic Inquiry and the Views Advanced in It." *Stem Publishing.* Online: http://www.stempublishing.com/authors/darby/PROPHET/02001E.html

———. "What the World Is; and How a Christian Can Live in It." *Stem Publishing.* Online: http://www.stempublishing.com/authors/darby/New8_95/38What_World_is.html

Davies, Jodie M. "Repression and Dissociation—Freud and Janet: Fairbairn's New Model of Unconscious Process." In *Fairbairn, Then and Now*, edited by Neil Skolnick and David E. Scharff, 53–69. Hillsdale, NJ: Analytic, 1998.

Dueck, Alvin C., and Kevin Reimer. *A Peaceable Psychology: Christian Therapy in a World of Many Cultures.* Grand Rapids: Brazos, 2009.

Edwards, Jonathan. *Charity and Its Fruits.* Edinburgh, UK: Banner of Truth Trust, 1998.

Ellis, William T. *Billy Sunday: His Life and Message.* Philadelphia, PA: John C. Winston Co., 1914.

Fairbairn, William Ronald Dodds. *Psychoanalytic Studies of the Personality*, 3–27. London: Tavistock, 1952.

———. "The Repression and the Return of Bad Objects (with Special Reference to the 'War Neuroses')." *British Journal of Medical Psychology* 19 (1943) 327–41.

Field, Marion. *John Nelson Darby: Prophetic Pioneer*. Surrey, UK: Highland, 2008.

Freeman-Attwood, Marigold. *Leap Castle: A Place and Its History*. Norwich, UK: Michael Russell, 2001.

Freud, Sigmund. "Mourning and Melancholia." In *The Standard Edition of the Complete Psychological Works of Sigmund Freud*, edited and translated by James Strachey, vol. 14, 237–58. London: Hogarth, 1917.

———. "Thoughts for the Times on War and Death." In *The Standard Edition of the Complete Psychological Works of Sigmund Freud*, edited and translated by James Strachey, vol. 14, 273–300. London: Hogarth, 1915.

Gavanas, Anna. *Fatherhood Politics in the United States: Masculinity, Sexuality, Race, and Marriage*. Champaign, IL: University of Illinois Press, 2004.

Grand, Sue. *The Reproduction of Evil: A Clinical and Cultural Perspective*. Hillsdale, NJ: Analytic, 2000.

Greenberg, Irving. *For the Sake of Heaven and Earth*. Philadelphia: Jewish Publication Society, 2004.

Greenburg, Jay R., and Stephen A. Mitchell. *Object Relations in Psychoanalytic Theory*. Cambridge, MA: Harvard University Press, 1983.

Gribben, Crawford. "Antichrist in Ireland: Protestant Millennialism and Irish Studies." In *Protestant Millennialism, Evangelicalism and Irish Society, 1790–2005*, edited by Crawford Gribben and Andrew Holmes, 1–30. New York: Palgrave Macmillan, 2006.

Gribben, Crawford, and Timothy Stunt. *Prisoners of Hope? Aspects of Evangelical Millennialism in Britain and Ireland, 1800–1880*. Waynesboro, GA: Paternoster, 2004.

Grotstein, James S. "Endopsychic Structure and the Cartography of the Internal World: Six Characters in Search of an Author." In *Fairbairn and the Origins of Object Relations*, edited by James S. Grotstein and Donald B. Rinsley, 112–50. New York: Other, 1994.

Hallie, Philip P. *Lest Innocent Blood Be Shed: The Story of the Village of Le Chambon and How Goodness Happened There*. New York: Harper, 1994.

Henzel, Ronald. *Darby, Dualism, and the Decline of Dispensationalism*. Tucson, AZ: Fenestra, 2003.

Hodgson, Peter C. *Hegel and Christian Theology: A Reading of the Lectures on the Philosophy of Religion*. New York: Oxford University Press, 2005.

Hoffman, Lowell. "Suffering, Glory and Outcomes in Psychotherapy." *Journal of Psychology and Christianity* 29.2 (2010) 130–40.

Hoffman, Marie T. "Incarnation, Crucifixion and Resurrection in Psychoanalytic Thought." *Journal of Psychology and Christianity* 29.2 (2010) 121–29.

———. *Toward Mutual Recognition: Relational Psychoanalysis and the Christian Narrative*. New York: Routledge, 2011.

Hoffman, Marie. T., and Lowell Hoffman. "Religion in the Life and Work of W. R. D. Fairbairn." In *Fairbairn and the Object Relations Tradition*, edited by Graham Clarke and David E. Scharff, 69–85. London: Karnac, 2014

Howell, Elizabeth. *The Dissociative Mind*. Hillsdale, NJ: Analytic, 2005.

James, William. *The Varieties of Religious Experience*. New York: Penguin, 1985.

Kim, Seyoon. "Salvation and Suffering According to Jesus." *Evangelical Quarterly* 68.3 (1996) 195–207.

Kimmel, M. *Manhood in America*. New York: Free, 1996.

Lake, Frank. *Clinical Theology: A Theological and Psychiatric Basis to Clinical Pastoral Care*. Lexington, KY: Emeth, 2006.

Lane, Belden. "Spirituality as the Performance of Desire: Calvin on the World as a Theatre of God's Glory." *Spiritus* 1 (2001) 1–30.

Lawrence, Tracey D. *The Greatest Sermons Ever Preached*. Nashville, TN: Thomas Nelson, 2005.

Levinas, Emmanuel. *Totality and Infinity: An Essay on Exteriority*. New York: Springer, 1980.

Macmurray, John. *Persons in Relation*. Atlantic Highlands, NJ: Humanities, 1961.

Makant, Mindy. "Re-membering Redemption: Bearing Witness to the Transformation of Suffering." PhD diss., Duke University Divinity School, 2012.

Malony, H. Newton and Samuel Southard. *Handbook of Religious Conversion*. Birmingham, AL: Religious Education, 1992.

Mangum, R. Todd. "High Hopes for 21st Century Dispensationalism: A Response to 'Hope and Dispensationalism: An Historical Overview and Assessment' (by Gary L. Nebeker)." Presentation to the Dispensational Study Group of the Evangelical Theological Society, Nashville, TN, 2000.

Marsden, George. *Fundamentalism and American Culture*. Oxford, UK: Oxford University Press, 2006.

———. *Understanding Fundamentalism and Evangelicalism*. Grand Rapids: Eerdmans, 1991.

Mendieta, Eduarto. *The Frankfurt School on Religion: Key Writings by the Major Thinkers*. New York: Routledge, 2004.

Mitchell, Stephen A. "Fairbairn's Object Seeking: Between Paradigms." In *Fairbairn, Then and Now*, edited by Neil Skolnick and David E. Scharff, 115–35. Hillsdale, NJ: Analytic, 1998.

Moltman, Jurgen. *The Crucified God*. Minneapolis, MN: Fortress, 1993.

Moody, Dwight. "Mother Moody's Prodigal Son." *Bible Truth Publishers*. Online: http://bibletruthpublishers.com/moodys-mothers-prodigal-son/dwight-l-moody/childrens-stories/dwight-l-moody/la89302

Moody, William R. *The Life of Dwight L. Moody*. New York: Fleming Revell, 1900.

Moorhead, James H. "Between Progress and Apocalypse: A Reassessment of Millennialism in American Religious Thought, 1800–1880." *The Journal of American History* 71.3 (1984) 524–42.

Nietzsche, Friedrich, and Walter Kaufmann. *The Gay Science: With a Prelude in Rhymes and an Appendix of Songs.* New York: Vintage, 1974.

Ortega, Mariana. "Wounds of Self: Experience, Word, Image, and Identity." *Journal of Speculative Philosophy* 22.4 (2008) 235–47.

Ostow, Mortimer. "Myth and Madness: A Report of a Psychoanalytic Study of Anti-Semitism." *International Journal of Psychoanalysis* 77 (1996) 15–31.

Perlman, Diane. "Intersubjective Dimensions of Terrorism and Its Transcendence." In *The Psychology of Terrorism, Vol. 1: A Public Understanding,* edited by Chris Stout, 17–47. Westport, CT: Prager, 2002.

Pfister, Oskar. "Letter from Oskar Pfister to Sigmund Freud, October 29, 1918." *International Psychoanalytic Library* 59 (1918) 63.

Pierson, George. *Yale: A Short History.* New Haven, CT: Yale University Press, 1976.

Planck, Karl A. "Broken Continuities: 'Night' and 'White Crucifixion.'" *Christian Century* (1987) 963.

Racker, Heinrich. "The Meanings and Uses of Countertransference." *Psychoanalytic Quarterly* 26 (1957) 303–57.

Rambo, Lewis. *Understanding Religious Conversion.* New Haven, CT: Yale University Press, 1993.

Reasoner, Vic. "The Hope of a Christian World: Part 2." *The Arminian Magazine* 25.2 (2007) 1–2.

Reis, Bruce. "Performative and Enactive Features of Psychoanalytic Witnessing: The Transference as the Scene of Address." *International Journal of Psychoanalysis* 90 (2009) 1359–72.

Ricoeur, Paul. *The Course of Recognition.* Cambridge, MA: Harvard University Press, 2005.

Rodgers, Julie. "Casualties in the Culture War." Personal Blog. Online: https://julierodgers.wordpress.com/2013/07/08/casualties-in-the-culture-war/

Rubens, Richard. L. "Fairbairn's Structural Theory." In *Fairbairn and the Origins of Object Relations,* edited by James S. Grotstein & Donald B. Rinsley, 151–73. New York: Other Press, 2000.

Rushing, D. Jean. "From Confederate Deserter to Decorated Veteran Bible Scholar: Exploring the Enigmatic Life of C. I. Scofield, 1861–1921." Online: http://dc.etsu.edu/etd/1380

Sandeen, Ernest. *The Roots of Fundamentalism: British and American Millenarianism, 1800– 1930.* Chicago: University of Chicago Press, 2008.

Sawyer, M. James. *Dispensationalism: An Introductory Survey.* Grand Rapids: Zondervan, 2006.

Scharff, David E., and Elinor Birtles. *From Instinct to Self: Selected Papers of W. R. D. Fairbairn, Volume I: Clinical and Theoretical Papers.* Northvale, NJ: Jason Aronson, 1994.

Schmidt, Alvin J. *How Christianity Changed the World.* Grand Rapids: Zondervan, 2004.

Schwartz, Scott C. "Medieval Antecedents of the Therapeutic Alliance." *Journal of the American Academy of Psychoanalysis* 27 (1999) 275–84.

Scofield, Cyrus Ingerson. *Rightly Dividing the Word of Truth.* Seattle, WA: CreateSpace Independent, 2014.

Shortt, J. G. "Toward a Reformed Epistemology and Its Educational Significance." Unpublished doctoral dissertation.

Singh, Devin. "Resurrection as Surplus and Possibility: Moltmann and Ricoeur." *Scottish Journal of Theology* 61 (2008) 251–69.

Skolnick, Neil and David E. Scharff. *Fairbairn, Then and Now.* Hillsdale, NJ: Analytic, 1998.

Stein, Ruth. "Vertical Mystical Homoeros: An Altered Form of Desire in Fundamentalism." *Studies in Gender and Sexuality* 4 (2003) 38–58.

Stern, D. N. *Interpersonal World of the Infant.* New York: Basic, 1985.

Stolorow, Robert D. "Heidegger's Nietzsche, the Doctrine of Eternal Return, and the Phenomenology of Human Finitude." *Journal of Phenomenological Psychology* 41 (2010) 106–14.

———. "Identity and Resurrective Ideology in an Age of Trauma." *Psychoanalytic Psychology* 26 (2009) 206–09.

———. "The Phenomenology of Trauma and the Absolutisms of Everyday Life: A Personal Journey." *Psychoanalytic Psychology* 16 (1999) 464–68.

Strozier, Charles. *Apocalypse: On the Psychology of Fundamentalism in America.* Eugene, OR: Wipf and Stock, 2002.

Sutherland, John D. *Fairbairn's Journey into the Interior.* London: Free Association, 1989.

Tchividjian, Boz. (2013). "Evangelical Sex Abuse Record 'Worse' than Catholic, says Billy Graham's Grandson Boz Tchividijian." *Huffington Post,* October 1, 2013. Online: http://www.huffingtonpost.com/2013/10/01/protestant-sex-abuse-boz-tchividijian_n_4019347.html

Terr, Lenore. "Childhood Trauma and the Creative Product: A Look at the Early Lives." *Psychoanalytic Study of the Child* 42 (1987) 545–72.

Terrell, C. Jeffrey. "A Discussion of Intentional Incarnational Integration in Relational Psychodynamic Psychotherapy." *Journal of Psychology and Christianity* 26.2 (2007) 159–65.

Tewksbury, Donald G. *The Founding of American Colleges and Universities before the Civil War: With Particular Reference to the Religious Influences Bearing upon the College Movement.* New York: Columbia University Press, 1932.

Trumbull, Charles G. *The Life Story of C. I. Scofield.* New York: Oxford University Press, 1920.

Turner, W. G. *Unknown and Well Known: A Biography of John Nelson Darby.* London: Chapter Two, 2006.

Ullman, Chana. *The Transformed Self: The Psychology of Religious Conversion.* New York: Plenum, 1989

Vale, Allison. *Hell House: And Other True Hauntings from around the World.* New York: Sterling, 2008.

Warfield, B. B. "The Emotional Life of Our Lord." In *The Person and Work of Christ*, edited by Samuel G. Craig, 93–148. Philadelphia: Presbyterian and Reformed, 1988.

Weremchuk, Max. *John Nelson Darby.* Neptune, NJ: Loizeaux, 1992.

Williams, David R. *James H. Brookes: A Memoir.* St. Louis, MO: Buschert, 1897.

Woodham-Smith, Cecil. *The Great Hunger: Ireland 1845–1849.* New York: Penguin, 1992.

Wright, N. T. *Surprised by Hope: Rethinking Heaven, the Resurrection, and the Mission of the Church.* New York: Harper Collins, 2008.

INDEX

and manic defenses, 102
and chauvinistic superiority,
103
and disintegration in personal
living, 109
true gospel, 98
Trumbull, Charles G., 77, 78

Ullman, Chana, 83
United Way, 3

Vale, Allison, 14
Vaughn, Samuel, 14

Warfield, Benjamin B., xi
Weremchuk, Max, 13, 18, 21, 22,
29
Williams, David R., 75, 76
witnessing
common usage of, 25
deconstructing, 26

present and future, 26
material and spiritual -26
individual and communal, 28
truncated view of, 29
of Jesus, 31
retraditioning, 31
at explicit and implicit levels, 32
of suffering and salvation, 60
and the horizontal split: evangelical neo-platonism, 98
healing the horizontal split, 99
Woodham-Smith, Cecil, 22
World Missionary Conference
(1910), 47
World War I, 5, 112
Wright, N. Thomas, 109
Wright, Ronald, 27

YMCA, 3, 81
YWCA, 3

Made in the USA
San Bernardino, CA
27 November 2016